# PLAYING BIGGER THAN YOU ARE

# PLAYING BIGGER THAN YOU ARE

## How to Sell Big Accounts Even if You're David in a World of Goliaths

**WILLIAM T. BROOKS**

**WILLIAM P. G. BROOKS**

WILEY

JOHN WILEY & SONS, INC.

Published by John Wiley & Sons, Inc., Hoboken, New Jersey.
Published simultaneously in Canada.

For general information on our other products and services or for technical support, please contact our Customer Care Department within the United States at (800) 762-2974, outside the United States at (317) 572-3993 or fax (317) 572-4002.

Wiley also publishes its books in a variety of electronic formats. Some content that appears in print may not be available in electronic books. For more information about Wiley products, visit our web site at www.wiley.com.

*Library of Congress Cataloging-in-Publication Data:*

Brooks, William T., 1945–2007
    Playing bigger than you are : how to sell big accounts even if you're David in a world of Goliaths / William T. Brooks, William P. G. Brooks.
        p. cm.
    ISBN 978-0-470-26035-7 (cloth)
    1. Selling–United States.    2. Small business–United States.    3. Selling–Terminology.

I. Brooks, William P. G. II. Title.
    HF5438.25.B7454 2010
    658.85–dc22

                                                                                    2009016552

Printed in the United States of America.

10  9  8  7  6  5  4  3  2  1

*This book is dedicated to the memory of its biggest advocate: my late father, Bill Brooks. It was a great pleasure to finish his final book. This book is also dedicated to The Brooks Group's committed staff members, without whom we never would have been able to "play bigger than we are." I'd also like to thank Jeff Davidson, who was a strong contributor to this book. Corrie Lisk-Hurst also deserves much credit for helping us publish this book, as she was instrumental in its development.*

# Contents

# Preface

There was only one thing Bill Brooks loved more than winning a big deal: hearing about another salesperson scoring an even bigger one (unless that person was competing for the same business, of course!).

He would have been thrilled to see this, his final work, come to fruition. *Playing Bigger Than You Are: How to Sell Big Accounts Even If You're a David in a World of Goliaths* is a book designed to show you how to win the biggest deals—and why you should go for them—no matter how small your operation is.

There are two kinds of Goliaths.

First, they're corporate behemoths (and even governments). A "small" expenditure by a Goliath might make your (or your company's) decade. But Goliaths are also your larger competitors—those who have bigger budgets, more staff resources, and demonstrated expertise in supplying products or services for giant corporations.

Take heart, all you Davids out there. This book outlines strategies and specific techniques that will help Davids—like you and us—gain opportunities with the Goliaths of business. This book is also about holding your own against your most sophisticated competitors by playing bigger than you are—and smarter than they are.

Too many small businesses pay attention to the reasons they *can't* make deals. This book forces readers to focus instead on the many reasons major corporations prefer smaller vendors and how to take advantage of this preference.

Everything in this book comes from experience. The Brooks Group is a small business by virtually any definition. By employing the ideas in this book, we've become the sales training provider of choice for many Goliaths. And we've beaten the Goliaths of our industry at the sales and sales management training game, time and time again.

How do you know if you're ready to sell to Goliaths? The answer to this question is in the first chapter of this book. You'll also learn why small businesses are uniquely qualified to sell to giants and find out not only which giants are the right ones to pursue but also where to find them.

Once you know whom you're pursuing, you need to know how they buy. Large corporations and government agencies often have complex and mysterious purchasing processes. This book discusses how corporate buyers make purchasing decisions and then turns to the topics of making successful sales presentations and eventually building on your successes.

If you're like many salespeople, you're preventing yourself from winning business from the giants, feeling daunted by the challenge. The middle chapters of this book will help you understand your own potential barriers to success, then show you how to position yourself properly to sell to giants.

The book investigates the ways Goliaths approach the process of making purchasing decisions. Many relatively recent shifts in the purchasing—or supply management—arena favor the Davids, if they understand how big companies think.

So, dive in. And start winning bigger accounts.

WILLIAM P. G. BROOKS
*Greensboro, North Carolina*

# About the Authors

Author of dozens of sales and sales management training, hiring, and selection articles, Will Brooks has worked with hundreds of companies across dozens of industries to help them improve their sales and sales management training, development hiring and retention practices. Having worked closely with his father, the late William T. "Bill" Brooks, for more than a decade, Will is now carrying forward many of Bill's time-tested and proven consulting theories and practices into the 21st century. Will continues to work with clients to develop and test new concepts and theories relative to the sales improvement arena. *Playing Bigger Than You Are* is a prime example of how looking at a sales strategy from a different angle can open opportunities for sales-driven companies of any size. The Brooks Group, Brooks's 20-person sales consulting company, currently works with several branches of the military, as well as many large, well-branded and nationally known companies to help them drive more sales, more strategically.

# Selling to Giants Will Transform Your Business

## The Business Is Out There, Waiting for You

Do you know that only a tiny percentage of the United States' 23 million small businesses currently serve the nation's largest corporations and organizations? That's really amazing, because small companies just like yours (and mine) offer products and services that huge organizations can—and do—buy! Unfortunately, the vast majority of us not only lack a system for successfully marketing to major corporations, we also don't display the personal confidence in our own abilities that will satisfy these corporations' requirements.

Most small businesses don't see it, but it's a fact: Your biggest competitors are seizing business opportunities that absolutely, positively could be ours.

If you're part of the sales effort for a small to midsized organization and you want to win the kind of big, profitable accounts that the giants in your industry do, this book is written for you.

**Read over the following statements and ask yourself if any of them resonate with you:**

- My biggest competitor has "least-risk" status in the minds of my prospects and customers.
- Our biggest competitors all have far more advertising dollars and marketing "waffle," and as a consequence, they are better positioned in the marketplace to win the bigger accounts than we are.
- My competitors have huge sales forces; they've cornered every market and built relationships, and I can't find a way in.
- My biggest competitor is always willing and able to compete on economy of scale and purchasing power, but I can't!

If you can identify with any of these statements, it's likely you are feeling overwhelmed, powerless, frustrated, and pressured when it comes to becoming the vendor of choice for the large accounts in your target market. Perhaps you're feeling as though the deck is stacked against you. So how can you compete?

Here's the short answer: It's all about positioning—your company's positioning and the positioning of your sales force. The slightly longer answer: You must be able to speak the language of corporate executives and buyers, understand and honor their rules and protocols, and possess an unwavering belief in the quality of the products or services you sell. Selling to the giants is not a game for the faint of heart, but if you play it right, you'll win big.

As you're carefully developing your overall sales strategy, consider some of the following reasons to market your company's products or services to giant corporations (and government entities):

- Larger, longer-term contracts make your cash flow and revenue more predictable.
- Fewer, but more valuable, contracts enable you to construct a stable business built on true core competencies.
- Your overhead is often lower when you are strategic about the accounts you pursue. A new contract will benefit from the systems and personnel dedicated to an existing agreement. Depending on your margin structure, supporting a large account may cost the same as supporting a smaller one.
- Enterprise-wide growth can be tremendous. A piece of business with one unit or division of a large company can lead to opportunities in other areas of the organization that you may not even target initially.
- Potential for referral-based business is huge. A recommendation from an executive at a giant corporation is worth its weight in gold!

# Many Giant Organizations Will Make It Easy for You

We often hear salespeople ask, "Do corporations help small, developing businesses seeking to do business with them?" The answer is a resounding "Yes!" Small domestic suppliers who can meet the challenge of serving as a key supplier to corporate giants will discover that many corporations exhibit strong commitment to employing and supporting qualified small suppliers.

**Corporations with strong small business supplier policies typically**

- Maintain a separate small business program office.
- Use external small business supplier directories.
- Provide information on goods and services purchased.
- Provide names and phone numbers of plant purchasing agents.
- Offer special assistance (management, financial, or technical) to small business suppliers.
- Maintain a directory or file on small business vendor capabilities.
- Set dollar or percentage goals for small business vendor use.
- Provide incentives to their purchasing staff to make use of small business suppliers.

Some corporations—Todd Shipyards and Honeywell, for example—have established aggressive small supplier procurement goals. Additionally, the federal government establishes formal goals for awarding prime contracts to small businesses. These goals typically provide a target for expected performance as well as an indicator of actual performance based on percent of purchases, contract dollar values, number of contracts, quantity of small vendors used, or a combination of these. Other goals might include metrics for visits to vendor sites, new vendors used, and contracts over a certain size awarded to small vendors.

According to a personal interview with a purchasing officer with FMC, a Chicago-based chemical manufacturer, "When dealing with small suppliers, a distinction must be made between qualified and qualifiable." What's the difference? Initially, many small businesses cannot meet the prospect's specifications; however, with some assistance from the larger corporation, they can become qualified suppliers.

Not all corporations are prepared or willing to make this effort, but purchasing coordinators in some more progressive corporations are willing to assist small suppliers by

- providing technical, managerial, and financial assistance.
- allowing longer lead times.
- arranging special payment terms.
- broadening product specifications.
- supplying information on pricing practices, bid preparation, production, sales, and servicing.
- assisting in developing a quality-control program.

## Small Business Purchasing Programs

Large corporations that develop and offer small business purchasing programs are demonstrating their commitment to increasing growth and marketing opportunities for smaller businesses like ours. Now the ball is in our court. We must be sure our small businesses provide maximum economic return, participating in capital formation and enhancing productivity.

In our area of North Carolina, we see firsthand how major corporate activities directly affect their respective business communities. FedEx is opening a major hub in Greensboro, and with its arrival comes a huge variety of industrial distribution opportunities and incentives for major corporations to relocate to the area. From the repercussions of the closing of Ralph Lauren's international fulfillment division in the Triad to the boon of the opening of a new HondaJet facility, we're seeing the ripple effect of major corporate activity on our community.

Corporate public relations officers know well that using small business suppliers helps offset some negative attitudes the public may have regarding a corporation's social responsibilities, especially in the economic environment of 2009. Large corporations and government agencies' involvement in small business can translate into investment opportunities for local residents, new construction and renovation of commercial property, boosts in purchasing and leasing of equipment, increased employment opportunities, and expansion of the local tax base, which will increase overall revenues to the municipality while easing the burden on individual taxpayers.

## There Are No Insiders: Everyone Starts as Strangers

I've heard it from countless entrepreneurs and salespeople: They know that what they have to sell is in demand, but they don't take the first step because they feel like outsiders. One salesperson I know named Matt told me about going to a trade show in Chicago and seeing one of his competitors smiling and joking with the corporate purchasing agent of a firm to which Matt wanted to sell. A few days later, Matt read a press release in his local newspaper detailing how another small firm in the next county grew 23 percent in one year by acquiring several large clients.

Matt's mental receptors were set to see, hear, and receive messages indicating that everyone knew everyone else. Consequently, he felt that efforts to win new business with major corporations would be fruitless because he didn't know the "right people." His story is not unique. Let's look at the fundamental question his story raises: Do others have inside connections they can bring to bear to help them experience superior sales results?

The answer is "yes and no."

It's "no" from the standpoint that everyone in this world starts off as a stranger to everyone else. Few of us were born well-connected in the business world. Instead, we have had to make most connections on our own. It's so easy to forget that the people we know in this world and the connections we have developed are largely the result of our own choices and actions.

Now for the "yes" answer. Some of your competitors will maintain an advantage over you simply because of whom they know. That's a fact. But let's return for a minute to Matt's situation and consider this: The one competitor he saw laughing and joking with a corporate purchasing agent must have invested her time calling on and getting to know that purchasing agent. Along the way, luck certainly could have played a part in her success. In the long run, however, those who are "wired" or have the inside connection usually earned it by allocating time, energy, and money toward the cultivation of key introductions, presentations, and follow-ups. You can do the same, can't you? Winning big business for your firm will be directly tied to how well you position yourself with key employees of giant corporations and to how well you manage the sales process with these people.

Every so often I hear about a middle or high school coach who makes it known that everyone who shows up at tryouts will make the soccer (or baseball, or cheerleading, or basketball) team. In fact, I've discovered that in the early weeks of the preseason, the teams usually have many more kids at practice than will be needed by the opening game. So what's a coach to do? Actually, he or she is betting on a sure thing: The final team roster will largely result from a self-selection process. Those athletes who truly want to play will stick it out all the way. The only players cut are those who cut themselves—they stop coming to practice and quit on their own.

Becoming a supplier to a giant corporation is also largely a self-selection process. To be successful, you have to show up—show up at their plant; visit them at trade shows; mail them relevant, valuable information; and speak to them by phone. As actor Woody Allen says, "Just showing up is 80 percent of everything."

One of my friends and colleagues posed a question at a regional meeting of the White House Conference on Small Business: "How many of you, right now, can tell me the name of at least one purchasing agent from a major corporation?" He said everyone in the room was silent. That sounds a lot like those folks were cutting themselves off of the team. Therefore, if you're willing to do your own research, make your own connections, and make the most of these efforts, your competition is limited to a few other brave souls.

## Why It Makes Sense to Pursue the Giants

A few years back at the Brooks Group, we hired a brilliant marketing expert named Mike Delaney. During his career, Mike has literally transformed companies such as Volvo Trucks NA and Unifi, to name just two, through skillful, research-based marketing. We figured that if we wanted to grow our own company, we could learn a lot from companies that are already huge. I'll be honest—he nearly drove us crazy with requests for data and countless interviews with staff and clients. But in the end, we had a corporate "A-ha!" moment that shaped how our company has grown since then: We discovered we had too many eggs in too few baskets.

Here's a brief overview of what we discussed:
- Too much of our business was generated by our founder through speaking engagements and personal contacts.
- We had one or two major (approximately million-dollar) clients every year, and they accounted for as much as half of our company revenue.

- We were spending—wasting might be a more appropriate term—a lot of time bidding on low-potential accounts, and when we won them we were investing a disproportionate amount of time and effort on servicing them.

That said, in my opinion, you don't have the time or money *not* to pursue big business, especially when you have the ability. I suspect you're probably like a lot of professionals in small business, and you're spending a lot of time working "in" your business, fighting fires, trying to maintain your hard-earned gains. You're interested in selling to the giants, but you just don't think you have the time, the ability, or the marketing dollars. Here's an old saying: It's time to stop working *in* your business and start working *on* your business.

Think about how much time you've spent over the last year being nickel-and-dimed by your clients, many of whom have budgets about the same size as yours. Every hour of staff time, every phone call or e-mail, and every conference about an account has monetary value—it's not just about the check you get from your client. But you know that already, right? At one point at The Brooks Group, we figured out that we were spending as much time servicing a low-dollar client as we were investing in one of our largest accounts. Yet if we had lost one of our biggest clients, we'd have been up the creek without a paddle.

In response, we made a conscious decision to focus several of our salespeople on earning big-dollar accounts: for example, one invests his time exploring private-sector potential, and another is dedicated to earning government business. This isn't to say we ignore our smaller clients—not by any means. Other salespeople are focused on building and maintaining our customer base with smaller and midsized organizations. It's just that we now manage our smaller accounts differently from our larger accounts so that our time is properly leveraged and all of our clients are best served.

So far, it's working beautifully. To get to this point, we had to take the time to work "on" our business, thinking strategically and making plans for getting to where we want to go. We had to stop being reactive, going after every piece of business. We committed to investing the time, effort, and financial resources to winning the kind of contracts we knew would be best for our company. In many ways, it's required a paradigm shift for us: to stop thinking about the immediate term and start looking long term; to hold out for business that earns us high margins versus business that would bring cash in the door at low margins. We now target very specific types of clients with a very precise message rather than marketing too broadly and watching for what sticks.

Why am I telling you all this? To make this point: It's a great idea to pursue business from the giant corporations and organizations, and I believe it should be part of your business strategy but not your entire business strategy. We now have a great mix of clients across many industry sectors—from industrial distribution to financial services to health care to the U.S. military. We have large contracts from small companies and small contracts from large ones. We have small contracts from small companies and large contracts from large ones, too. What we've done is figure out where our "sweet spots" are and concentrate on them; our clients are well-served and happy, and we're satisfied with the returns, no matter how large the organization we're serving.

## Why Some People Should Not Sell to the Giants

Now that we've looked at some of the many benefits of selling to large corporations and government entities, I think I'd better caution those of you who really *shouldn't* try to sell to the giants:

- Are you extremely risk tolerant? Selling to the giants requires a lot of time, effort, and other resources. Furthermore, the payoff is almost never immediate.

- Are you truly trying to grow your business, or are you happy with your current size? Be careful: 20 percent client erosion per year isn't out of the ordinary.

- Are you willing and able to be smart and strategic about cultivating large accounts? It takes patience and business savvy, plus you've got to target your goals with everything you've got.

- Do you believe it's worth it? If you don't believe in the potential of big clients, most likely you'll fail. Therefore, you'll be better served by continuing to do what's worked for you before.

- Do you have a strong team you can rely on? Selling to the giants requires a cohesive team effort—you've got to be 100 percent confident in your lineup.

- Is project management one of your stronger areas? Giant accounts have serious complexities and require high levels of responsiveness. You must be capable of developing plans and keeping all the program components moving smoothly.

- Are you willing to delegate and trust your team to deliver? There are simply too many moving parts in your business to try to do it all yourself. Selling to the giants requires tight coordination and excellent teamwork.

If you answered "no" to all of the above questions, I recommend putting your eggs in other baskets. It is certainly possible to run a successful business without having large corporate accounts., but I will challenge you with one very important question: If you answered "yes" to *all* of these questions, how effectively do you think you can grow and maintain your business as it stands now? It's a harsh question, but one worth asking yourself.

If you had a few "no" answers, then those are the areas I'd recommend focusing on as you move your business forward. If you know you're not the best project manager in the world, consider hiring an experienced, knowledgeable project manager.

If you don't think you can be smart and strategic about cultivating large accounts, can you be smart and strategic about the rest of your business? What can you do to ensure that you stay ahead of the curve, no matter where your revenue comes from?

## How Selling to the Giants Will Affect Your Business

If you're reading this book, I'm assuming you're either leaning toward or have already made the decision to pursue the giants in your target market. It's all well and good to want to become a supplier to a corporate giant or government organization, and one single contract from such an agency can be worth millions. But—and this is a biggie—if you're not organized enough to support and service a large-scale account, you'll lose your shirt. And—yes, there's more—if you plan to win large accounts, you'd better be thinking about staffing up to support them, not waiting until after they're won.

You need to be planning *now* for what you'll need in 18 months, when you win that first big account and you become the supplier of choice for a multimillion (or multibillion) dollar enterprise. For most of us, that doesn't mean turning down smaller dollar business to focus solely on selling to a giant. It means being strategic about allocating time, effort, and other resources to

- the kinds of business that have gotten you where you are today.
- the kinds of business you want to earn tomorrow (or 18 months from now).

Ideally, you developed a complete business plan when you started your company. However, few small businesses made the effort to establish a comprehensive plan for marketing, financing, and human resources before they hit the ground running. Often the terms "business plan" and "sales and marketing plan" are used interchangeably, but a sales and marketing plan is really a part (albeit the most important) of the strategic business plan. If you can't describe what market(s) you will serve, how you will generate revenue, and how long it will take, then everything else is just about meaningless.

Underestimating the time and effort required to market to corporate giants is a classic mistake would-be suppliers make. It truly may take 18 months or more (on average) from the first moment you make contact to close a contract with a major corporation. That's right—almost two years. Doesn't it make sense that your current business model will have to change if you want to win favored-supplier status with a large organization?

## Getting Your Ducks in a Row

Are you ready to sell to the giants? If you're going to pursue business from giant corporations and government agencies, be sure you have your operational ducks in a row. Large corporations expect you to be organized and efficient and to be able to meet quality and delivery expectations without significant glitches. An essential part of doing this is organizing your team—from sales through operations and on to customer service—with these expectations in mind.

Many companies make the mistake of allowing functional groups in their organization to exist essentially independently rather than integrating their marketing, sales, and service efforts. This is a surefire way to alienate customers and create an unhappy workforce. The example I always like to use is a car dealer who advertises the dealership's service quality by assuring customers that the service on their new cars will be "done correctly, the first time, every time." And he really believes it. But when *your* vehicle goes in for service, you get far less than what the dealership's advertising promised.

Your prospects and customers receive a promise about how they'll be treated and what results they can expect from working with you. When you promise them something, they have the ex-pectation that you'll fulfill your promise. The car dealer promised service that was correct, the first time and every time. Customers expected that of your service appointment, but their experience didn't live up to your expectation!

The words "promise," "expectation," and "experience" show how tightly your marketing, sales, and service efforts must be in-tegrated. Definitions of marketing and sales are no doubt clear to you, but let me clarify that service relates to delivery, tech-nical support, operations, customer service, or any other group of people who interact with your customers during and after the sale.

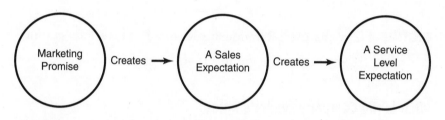

**FIGURE 1.1**   Disconnected Promise-Expectation-Experience Chain

When there's a disconnect between any two (or all three) components in the promise-expectation-experience chain, you have a major problem. No one is talking to anyone else in the organization. Prospects who meet with your salespeople have expectations that could either be unmet or wildly exceeded, and customers who do buy from you could either be disappointed or thrilled with the service they receive. The result of all this? An organization that faces finger-pointing, denial, reduced cash flow, client dissatisfaction, and possibly even failure.

In contrast, if your organization is smart about integrat-ing your marketing, sales, and service components, you'll have an unbroken promise-expectation-experience chain. In the ideal world, the three components overlap and are totally integrated.

**FIGURE 1.2**   The Ideal Relationship among Promise-Expectation-Experience

## What Is the Company Leader's Role?

If you're the company's leader, your biggest business development role is driving the long-term sales and marketing effort. Remember, the purpose of marketing should be to plan for your company's long-range future, not to sell a few more widgets here and there. But isn't it far too easy to complete the tasks that bring immediate satisfaction while ignoring the less-desirable tasks that produce less-obvious short-term results? I think this is especially true if you're an entrepreneur—it's just part of your makeup.

If your company is doing reasonably well right now, you may forget what it was like when you weren't sure where the next contract was coming from. Or maybe you're in the opposite position—you remember all too well what it feels like when you're not sure you can make payroll, so you're convinced you have to be 100-percent in control of every aspect of your business, leaving nothing to chance.

Trusting your staff to think for themselves, embrace change, and move the company forward often feels like a risky move. Talk about variables! But if you don't trust your staff to do the right things, not only will you do more work than you should do by yourself and over-control your team, you'll also guarantee they become de-motivated, uncreative, and unable to function as a team. I've seen it firsthand: it's a recipe for disaster.

Remember what I said a few paragraphs ago: It takes an average of 18 months from initial contact with a large corporation to the establishment of a solid contractual agreement. Large corporations are notoriously slow by small business standards.

I encourage you to plan where you want your company to be in one year, three years, and five years. All the corporate giants go through this drill—and for good reason. Your long-range plan should include specific, measurable goals for products and services you want to offer, along with the number of employees and amount of space you'll need to experience reasonable and realistic growth. Next, map out and follow strategies to meet these goals.

Setting sales and marketing goals won't guarantee success, but evidence strongly supports the theory that you are much more likely to meet goals when they are clearly defined and regularly reviewed for status and relevance purposes.

If you have a small staff and no marketing help at all, you become the director of sales and marketing by default. Be prepared to dedicate at least 20 to 25 percent of your time on these activities; however, you should also delegate support activities such as research and organization to someone else. Twenty percent of your time equals at least eight hours per week, 400 hours per year, at a minimum. That looks like a lot, doesn't it? Not if you see it as the most critical 20 percent of your time!

The single best way to increase your sales and marketing effectiveness is to free your time by delegating tasks that can be assigned to someone else. If your company employs more than 12 people, you should have at least one full-time marketing person. I'm not talking about a low-paid marketing assistant who also answers the telephone and makes Microsoft Publisher fliers for trade shows. I'm talking about a knowledgeable, experienced professional who can help you move your company upward and onward. And just because you hire a marketing person doesn't mean you are off the hook—you should still be investing good quality time every week in the marketing effort.

I know—I've been there. Delegating authority to others to complete important tasks sometimes feels unnatural. As leaders of companies, our own hard work has built our organizations to where they are now, and we can't resist wanting to keep our finger on as many functions as possible. Let me tell you, though, that in the long run, your sales effectiveness will live or die with your ability to delegate.

## What's the Salesperson's Role?

If you're a salesperson for a small business, your primary role is to position yourself so that you are able to sell to the giants. What does this mean? It means you have to be confident enough to handle yourself with composure no matter whether you're talking with a purchasing agent or a company CEO. You have to be perceived as an expert in your field and as someone who adds value to the large corporation and its personnel.

As I've already said, many large organizations make it relatively easy to be considered as a supplier. But that's only part of your battle. You have the hard—but potentially very rewarding—job of making the most of the opportunity. Of course, there are many large corporations your company could serve that *don't* make it particularly easy for small suppliers. They feel that smaller vendors are "riskier." That's not to say the business can't be won, but winning it takes patience, a systematic approach, and strong personal positioning. In fact, most of the rest of this book is about positioning yourself effectively with the giants—getting in front of the right people with the right message at the right time, which is the essence of successful selling at any level, actually.

## What's Your Operation Like?

Many things about small businesses make working with them attractive to the giants. As a general rule, small businesses like yours (and ours)

- are far more flexible than larger firms.
- are more responsive than larger suppliers.
- have a shorter innovation to production cycle.
- have close-knit, effective project teams.
- avoid bureaucratic delays and have true accountability.

Many giant corporations like to deal with smaller suppliers because they feel more important to the smaller firms; they believe—usually correctly—that they'll get more prompt service and more attention than they would from a larger supplier. Your job in selling to giant corporations and government agencies is to find out what, when, and how each organization will buy what you sell. After the giant expresses interest in buying from your firm, you'll need to prove them right, giving them all of the service and attention they expect (and more!). Although each company buys in its own way, in general, the giants will want to know the following:

- You have specific quality control measures in place.
- You have key points of contact in place at all critical points of interface with your firm. These contacts should be easily reachable.
- You have smart, solid contingency plans in place.
- You have quality-assurance structures in place for any other suppliers with which you're partnering.

- You're in controlled-growth mode, not out-of-control growth mode.
- You have the technological sophistication to segregate their data and information from that of other clients.
- You have the technology—and tech support—to facilitate real-time collaboration.
- You have the ability to be confidential.

Of course, this list isn't comprehensive; these are just a few of the most common things I've observed. Some companies may have more stringent criteria for their suppliers than others.

## How Are Your Finances?

Small businesses are sometimes seen as higher-risk vendors simply because they don't have the financial sophistication, stability, or years in business that larger firms may have. One of the best recommendations I have is that you establish a strong relationship with a reputable lender. You should have a clear idea of what types and amounts of loans you'd be eligible for and do what you can to prequalify for them. If you don't already have one, establish a credit line with a solid, reputable financial organization.

Think ahead on your finances. This will give you a cushion in tight times and the ability to invest in anticipation of future business. I just recently heard a CEO complain that he was having to jump through hoops to get financing to buy a new facility. His corporation has been on a growth trajectory and is projected to bring in $20 million in revenue this year—in a down economy, his revenues are up. But especially in today's economic climate, banks are increasingly careful about whom they loan money to. Even if you have good credit—as this CEO does—it can take a lot of time and effort to get the money you need to take your business to the next level.

Many giant corporations have expectations of their small suppliers, too. They don't want to tie their success in any way to a vendor who's not 100-percent reliable and in business for the long term. You must have your finances in order, have a long-term strategic plan for your firm's viability, and be able to communicate effectively about how your solutions will contribute to the giant's overall financial profitability.

## Do You Have a Sales Process?

Whether your sales team includes 20 people or just you and a sales assistant, following a linked, sequential sales process is essential to your success at selling to the giants (or to anyone, for that matter). Here at The Brooks Group, we teach and practice the IMPACT Selling® System, and of course, I think it's the best one around. If you're not using a selling system, start using one as soon as possible. It doesn't have to be ours; most reputable systems have elements in common and will achieve the same goal: being systematic about how you approach sales.

A selling system helps you know where you are in the sales process and what to do next. That may sound simple, but *not* knowing where you are or where to go next is one of the most common mistakes salespeople make. We've seen it far too many times, so we're strong believers in following the system. Any Brooks Group salesperson can tell you exactly where he or she is in the sales process with a prospect or client any time you ask. Following a system lets them plan their time and invest their energy for greatest effect.

## Moving Ahead

If you've done your research and put the pieces into place, you're ready to begin pursuing the giants. (Odds are that you're *already* pursuing them but quite possibly not as effectively as you could be.) In the chapters that follow, I'm going to give you the best guidance I can about how to position yourself, your company, and your products or services to be most appealing to large corporations and government agencies. And I'll also give you some tactical tips on when and how to approach the giants to increase your odds of success.

## Critical Points from This Chapter

- How can you compete? It's all about positioning. You must be able to speak the language of corporate buyers and other executives, understand and honor their rules and protocols, and possess an unwavering belief in the quality of the products or services you sell.

- We often hear salespeople ask, "Do corporations help small, developing businesses seeking to do business with them?" The answer is a resounding "Yes!"

- Large corporations that offer small business purchasing programs are demonstrating their commitment to increasing growth and sales opportunities for businesses like ours. Now the ball is in our court. We must provide maximum economic return, participating in capital formation and enhancing productivity.

- The only players cut are those who cut themselves—they stop coming to practice and quit on their own.

- You don't think you have the time, ability, or marketing dollars to sell to the giants? It's time to stop working *in* your business and start working *on* it.

- It's a great idea to pursue business from giant corporations and organizations, and we believe it should be a part of your business strategy, *but not your entire business strategy*.

- If you're not organized to support and service a large-scale account, you'll lose your shirt. And if you plan to win large accounts, you'd better be thinking about staffing up to support them, not waiting to do so until after they're won.

- Underestimating the time and effort required to sell to corporate giants is a classic mistake would-be suppliers make. It takes 18 months or more (on average) to close a contract with a major corporation.

# Small Businesses Are Uniquely Qualified to Sell to Giants

## Suppliers Just Like You Are Needed

Many smaller businesses, from manufacturers to construction contractors and professional service providers, could be serving as key suppliers to corporate giants and government agencies. But most small business leaders like us don't realize that there's a tremendous variety of opportunities out there, ripe for the picking. Most of us make the mistake of focusing only on a company's end product when considering our market potential with the company. We assume a company that makes widgets is only interested in suppliers who can make widget parts, and because we don't sell widgets parts, we don't consider the company a qualified prospect for us. Luckily, that couldn't be farther from the truth!

Take a company like Polaroid. At different times, Polaroid has sought service vendors in transportation, construction, data entry, and even snow removal. They use suppliers of office furniture, electronic equipment, chemicals, and fuels on a routine basis. Chesebrough-Pond's has used diverse vendors from a hose and gasket manufacturer to a pharmaceutical lab. Hewlett-Packard spends billions annually on indirect services, including labor, technology, sales and marketing, travel, meetings and events, and business services.

Federal, state, and local governments are also sources of large contracts, and many government agencies give preference to small businesses. If you'd told me 25 years ago that our company would be providing sales training to military recruiters, I'd have been surprised, but some of our largest clients at The Brooks Group are the U.S. Air Force Reserve and the Air National Guard, which train thousands of folks every year on everything from technical topics to leadership skills. Recruiting new Reservists and Guard members is a specialized job that really looks a lot like selling. We modified our IMPACT Selling System for these military recruiting purposes, and it's achieved stellar results—the Air Force Reserve beat its recruiting targets for eight years in a row after implementing our system.

Would it ever have occurred to you that the military would want to outsource sales training? Countless opportunities are out there that might surprise you at first but that will seem perfectly reasonable once you've let the idea sink in. The following list includes some of the major, more obvious areas of opportunity for small firms. These are just a few examples of many, but I'm sure you'll get the gist.

Accounting services
Advertising and public relations
Architecture
Barcoding
Building management
Computer hardware and
    software
Construction
Data storage and retrieval
Demolition, disposal, recycling
Electronic data interchanges
Engineering services
Environmental services
Food services
Graphics and technical
    communication
Health services planning

Industrial design
Landscaping
Legal services
Management consulting
Noise impact studies
Office furniture and
    supplies
Peripheral equipment
Protective equipment and
    clothing
Repair services
Research
Security
Temporary labor
Transportation
Video production
Warehousing

Don't assume a corporate giant can't use your services just because those services are not directly related to the corporation's end products. Contractors, professional service companies, and manufacturers who don't recognize that there are wide-ranging opportunities with major companies may be seriously limiting their potential. It will take you some prospecting to identify the right corporate contacts, but the potential rewards certainly justify the effort.

## What Are the Giants Looking For?

Now that you understand that what you sell has value for large corporations and government entities, let's take a closer look at what would motivate a giant to buy your products or services. A few years back, we conducted an experiment on customer buying motives, surveying 100 experienced purchasing managers and 100 inexperienced ones about how much of several products they would buy from various vendors. The results were amazingly consistent: *not a single* experienced buyer picked the lowest-priced vendor. The reasons they gave for choosing the higher-priced vendor was either "history of delivery" or "quality standards of the vendor." (Interestingly, the vast majority of the inexperienced buying group picked the vendor who was mathematically the lowest priced.) If you can't guarantee these two things—delivery and quality—don't even bother trying to get business from the giants.

### Delivery. On-Time. No Exceptions.

We did a study of purchasing functions and activities at 64 firms, and we discovered that in 70.2 percent of the cases, a delivery problem was the trigger event that caused a firm to drop one of its suppliers. All too often, we hear that suppliers quote a delivery date and even confirm the date, but never call even once to say that there is a problem in their production schedule and that actual delivery might be 15, 30, or 45 days after the target date. *A delivery problem is virtually always the reason you will lose a sale to one of your existing customers.*

## A Special Note about Sustainability

Words such as "climate change" and "sustainability" aren't just buzzwords for big businesses. Huge corporations in all sectors—from HSBC Bank to HP to Wal-Mart—are paying attention to issues of social and environmental responsibility. According to recent surveys we've seen, somewhere around half of large corporations have formal sustainability policies for managers, designers, and purchasing personnel to follow, and that number is likely to continue growing.

Why? Some corporate officers have a genuine philosophical commitment to reducing their carbon footprints. Energy efficiency yields big savings, especially as energy costs increase. Many business leaders say that focusing on sustainability has increased innovation at their firms. Government regulations and environmental groups are putting significant pressure on corporations to "go green." And last, but not least, going green seems to be a serious market differentiator for corporations.

Whatever the reason, it's good news for you: It opens up new avenues for innovative products and services. And if you're a green supplier, you have a leg up on your competition!

Although developing and cementing small vendor/large corporation partnerships is usually desirable for the parties involved, corporate trust and confidence in suppliers often break down because purchasing departments often find out about late shipments only when the goods don't arrive as scheduled. Many buyers spend an inordinate amount of time on the phone trying to run down what happened to a shipment and when it will be arriving.

One purchasing manager lamented, "We don't seem to be able to train suppliers to call us first." The situation occurs when suppliers over-promise in their deal to close a sale. Corporate purchasing departments have seen this happen time and time again and don't enjoy being taken advantage of. That said, I wouldn't recommend putting yourself in a situation in which you have to make that call. Some customers will find another supplier immediately, costing you the sale—because they have to. Your clients order your products or services because they want and/or need them—and need them on time.

It's a fact: Your customers really don't care why you missed the delivery date. They only know two things: (1) it isn't there, and (2) it is your fault. Nor do your customers want to know how good your reason is for missing the delivery date to which you committed. They just want to know exactly how you're going to get the products or services they need to the place they need to be at the soonest possible moment. If you can't provide this information, they'll look for other sources, and you may not get another chance to win their business.

Another complaint I've heard a lot is that clients are often forced to commit additional dollars to warehousing and safety stocks to compensate for their suppliers' slow deliveries. That's one of the worst situations you can be in, because not only are you costing your clients money for the products or services you provide, but you're also costing them additional dollars they could be using elsewhere more productively. I understand that some suppliers get stuck because they don't have sufficient inventory on hand to meet their promised delivery dates, but others simply lack adequate internal planning to deliver as promised. Don't be one of those firms!

Make no mistake: If you can't resolve these issues and develop backup plans, you should *not* be pursuing business with the giants. The absolute best suppliers I know work closely with their clients to ensure that delivery of needed goods is just-in-time (JIT). There's a supply chain logistics firm here in North Carolina (and there are many others globally) that has made its fortune helping large organizations do just that—ensuring that the products and parts they need are available exactly when required by establishing a network of warehouses and sophisticated computer systems nationwide so that items are available within hours of request. It may be just this kind of responsiveness that your giant accounts require, so be prepared.

## Quality. No Ifs, Ands, or Buts

Corporate giants today do business with qualified suppliers from around the world. They go wherever necessary to get the price, quality, delivery, and other terms they need to purchase successfully. But given the choice, most American corporations would prefer to do business with domestic suppliers—the closer, the better. This is true because there are many, many hidden costs of using overseas suppliers, including the following:

- Identifying potential suppliers
- Certifying suppliers to be used
- Tooling and machining to make parts
- Agent commissions, brokerage fees, and other "middleman" expenses
- Warehousing
- Shipping, insurance, and inventory costs
- Export fees, documentation, and extra paperwork
- Shipping, unloading, freight, delivery
- Customs fees, import fees, duties, and surcharges
- Foreign exchange rates

But many domestic corporations are going beyond U.S. borders to find qualified suppliers. Why? Because there's an unfortunately widely held perception that domestic suppliers can't meet the quality levels that large corporations require.

One buyer we talked to noted that "the supplier base in this country has a long way to go to understand the Japanese level of quality." A purchasing VP at another company commented, "All things being equal, we would prefer to source domestically. It is a matter of convenience, language, and culture. But all things are not equal, and we have to find the best available sources if we are to remain successful."

We often hear purchasing managers and other executives say things like, "Too many of our suppliers are complacent about quality. They talk about improving quality, but it's not reflected in the goods we receive." Estimates of total quality errors per shipment range from 10 to 20 percent, depending on the industry, but that means that one to two out of 10 items your customers are receiving don't meet their standards of quality.

Our studies have shown that quality can be the single most important reason a buyer will commit to purchasing what you sell. If you can demonstrate that your products and services meet your prospects' quality requirements consistently and at a fair price, there will be little that can hold you back. It's worth noting here that although most people will tell you that quality means "best," literally, this isn't always the case. Let me explain. Actually, a quality product or service is one that conforms to your customer's standards and expectations. Quality means the right stuff, not the best stuff. Quality is the correct stuff for your prospect's requirements and needs, not the best stuff made.

When you can guarantee an agreed-on level of quality, corporate buyers are freed from having to perform this function, reducing their through-put time in producing their final product. Supplier-based quality control programs also reduce corporations' labor, inventory, and returned shipment costs. If you are able not only to guarantee the delivery dates of shipments but also to ensure consistent quality of those shipments, you have a distinct advantage over your competitors—who often do not or cannot. Luckily for you, smaller businesses like yours can control those critical factors far better than larger corporations.

## What Else Are They Looking For?

On-time delivery and quality are the non-negotiables when dealing with large corporations. But they're not the only factors that go into becoming a key supplier to the giants. The past 15 to 20 years have brought a revolution in purchasing and a rise of supply chain economics. Large organizations—if they're smart—are looking enterprise-wide for solutions, savings, and efficiencies. As a result, the purchasing function has become far more strategic than in the past, and departments throughout the organization are changing.

Although there are certainly purchasing personnel who are tasked with placing day-to-day orders and fulfilling other clerical functions, the overall purpose of the purchasing department has become more strategic. In many companies, it's not even called "Purchasing" anymore; it's called "Supply Management" or "Supply Chain Management," depending on the level of its influence. This evolution from tactical to strategic functions means that other changes have occurred:

- **Purchasing/Supply Management is involved in more company-wide decisions.** With a shift to enterprise-wide thinking, decisions about health care, fleets, temporary/contract labor, travel, and other areas that were handled by other departments (or by each division) in the past are often now handled by a central supply management or purchasing department.

- **Purchasing/Supply Management executives report directly to the CEO.** In the past, the purchasing department often was subordinate to the finance or operations department, but today, there's a vice president or even C-level executive over the purchasing/supply management function. This executive has a seat at the CEO's table and is intimately involved in developing company strategy and executing it.

- **Collaboration, not hard-nosed negotiation, is the rule.** This isn't to say that the giants don't want the best price, but most don't buy *purely* on lowest price. Most are looking for suppliers who are willing to be collaborators and partners, not just order-takers.

- **Real-time visibility into the supply chain via Web-based tools is the norm.** You'd better be prepared to share your data, and the more you can share in real time, the better. Virtually every major corporation uses some type of enterprise resource planning (ERP) tool, as well as a customer relationship management (CRM) tool. Many have implemented complete supply chain management (SCM) applications that integrate data from every part of the supply chain.

As you can see—and you may already have experienced—this shift from a tactical to strategic view has had significant effects on suppliers. Corporate giants have far different expectations of their suppliers than they did as little as 15 years ago, and increasingly sophisticated technologies have been at the core of these changes. Here are a few of the expectations you'll find that giants and large government agencies have of their suppliers:

- **Vendor Value Analysis.** Value analysis is continually researching, refining, and adapting products and services so they can be built faster, delivered less expensively, last longer, or improve in some other measurable way. Suppliers who are able to assist large companies' purchasing agents not only by supplying needed goods and services—but by contributing to value analysis—will likely become favored suppliers.

- **Real-Time Collaboration.** Believe it or not, fax and e-mail are just too slow nowadays. Giant corporations have sophisticated, smart supply chain systems (like those from i2 Technologies, Red Prairie, and others) that enable real-time materials planning, inventory management, order and delivery status, and much more. Web-enabled communities that suppliers, buyers, manufacturers, and service providers can access ensure real-time, back-and-forth collaboration from initial planning to after-delivery service.

- **Just-in-Time Inventory Systems.** Nearly every product that gets made sits in a warehouse for at least some time. The goal behind JIT inventory management is to have the least amount of inventory warehoused but still be able to fulfill orders on demand. It is a complex science that, if done right, yields significant cost savings. If you sell products or parts, you must be able to show your giant clients you can help them in this area.

- **Maintaining Reserve and Replacement Parts.** Successful suppliers recognize that in addition to meeting contract specifications, they should also be prepared to be the source for spare parts and service for equipment they're supplying. This doesn't apply just to manufacturing—in our business, it could mean overnighting backup copies of training manuals to a client representative or reviewing a difficult personnel assessment with a hiring manager.

- **Competitive, Justifiable Pricing.** If lowest price were the only reason anyone bought anything, we wouldn't need salespeople, would we? Remember our research with experienced, trained buyers? They never buy solely on price. The price they were after was one that was "justifiable." They want something else—delivery and/or quality—with a price that would make it easy for them to justify *not* buying from the cheapest vendor.

*Purchasing* magazine surveys its readers regularly to determine the major problems they face. There are a variety of concerns, but a few emerge quite consistently, virtually every year:

- Meeting worldwide competition
- Keeping lead times short, quality high, and unit prices down

- Reducing paperwork and paper shuffling
- Obtaining favorable long-term price commitments
- Balancing price, quality, and the desire for long-term supplier relations
- Getting quality material at a competitive price as scheduled
- Balancing incoming sales against forecasted production
- Reducing production parts and operating supplies to achieve minimum inventories
- Identifying, evaluating, and breaking in new vendors and suppliers
- Expediting critical orders
- Orienting supply to JIT systems
- Coping with price fluctuations in long-term contracts
- Managing nonconforming shipments

If your goal is to serve as a key supplier to a giant corporation or government entity, your mission should be clear: Make the purchasing agent's job easier.

## Small Businesses Are Uniquely Qualified to Meet These Requirements

At The Brooks Group, we've come to the realization that we aren't the perfect solution for every prospect. It's just a fact. However, we believe that what we offer is of tremendous value to specific prospects in certain niches. One of our salespeople, Richard, often refers to The Brooks Group as a "boutique" sales and sales management training firm, one that is "tightly—but deeply—niched." We've learned over more than 30 years what our primary strengths are, and what types of clients we will best serve.

In recent years, we've done training for several of the United States' largest automotive and equipment mortgage companies, helping their salespeople be more effective at selling their mortgage services to dealerships. By customizing programs for each of these clients, we developed a deep understanding of the issues they face, and we now have a big-picture view of the industry as a whole. This industry knowledge is what has earned us repeat business from our existing clients and new business from new prospects. We bring unique value to the table because we have a very specific, targeted understanding of what it takes to sell auto and equipment mortgages.

But there's more. Most of these clients are large corporations, or divisions of large corporations. In the world of sales training companies, we're a small to midsize sales training firm. How did we get our first big financial services account? When we *didn't* have depth of industry knowledge, what *did* we offer that was appealing? A few things:

- **Responsiveness.** A large corporation knows that they are a large source of revenue for you. Corporate personnel like knowing that the business is critical to you. How much more likely are you to return a call to a client that makes up 20 percent of your annual revenue than one who makes up only .5 percent? Yes, all clients are important, and the .5 percent might grow into a larger one. But let's be realistic here. If your single largest client wants something from you, you will jump through hoops to give it to them.
- **Flexibility.** Larger sales training firms are far less likely to customize programs for their clients, and if they do, it will cost a lot. Customizing sales training programs is a way of life for us, and it's something most of our clients have benefited from. Our smaller size—and fewer "moving parts" enables us to make changes rapidly and inexpensively.
- **Speed.** We're small, but we have exactly the personnel we need, and we have the financial stability to bring resources to bear if needed. If a client needs a simple sales training

program tomorrow, odds are we can have a trainer in place and on a plane within hours. If a client needs a fully customized sales and sales management curriculum, we can complete it as fast as that client can provide personnel to collaborate with us on it.

- **Innovation.** Smaller firms almost always have a faster innovation-implementation cycle than larger ones. Sometimes innovation comes by accident—in trying to anticipate a customer's needs or even making a mistake on a job. Other times innovation is intentional.

## Choosing Your Battles

If you're going to win, and win big at selling to the giants, you've got to be specific and detailed about what your goal is. The rest of this book will be about the tactical aspects of selling these accounts, but there's no use in talking tactics if you don't have a focus for your plans. Setting your own goals based on your ideals is a great starting point for getting the results you want, so let's take a few minutes here to review the components of strong goals:

- A goal is a specific target. It's something you believe is worth doing and you feel you can do. It's something you can fix your aim on, concentrating only on the target. The more specific, the better your chances of reaching it.
- A goal is achievable. It's not vague or unrealistic. People often set goals so high, and place target dates so far out into the future that they have no hope of reaching them. A good goal is one that causes you to stretch all of your abilities, but one you're reasonably confident you can reach.
- A goal is a present reality, and it has a timetable. Your short- and intermediate-term objectives should be directly related

to your long-term goals and have specific timeframes for completion. That way, everything you do tomorrow will have an impact on where you're going to be five years from now.

- A goal is a promise you make to yourself. We have an easier time keeping promises we make to other people than we do keeping promises we make to ourselves. This is partly because others actually hold us to our promises, but we tend to cut ourselves some slack. I recommend considering your goals to be formal promises to yourself and keeping these promises with the same tenacity you'd keep a promise to your dearest loved one.

- A goal is a stepping stone. Each time you reach a goal, you're at a place where you can set bigger and better goals and expand your horizons.

If you're going to sell to the giants, you need to be diligent about setting realistic but challenging goals for yourself and holding yourself accountable for following through. Let me suggest a few questions to get you started setting your big account goals:

- What products or services do you offer that would be ideal for a giant customer?
- What are five large corporations or government agencies from which you most want to get business?
- Do any large corporations have divisions or business units that have a strong presence in your part of the country?
- How much capacity does your existing infrastructure— personnel, equipment, finances, and so on—have? How much can you realistically grow in six months? One year? Five years?

- Are you (or your salespeople) capable of being taken seriously by executives at giant corporations? How are you positioned?

Now that you've set your goals for selling to the giants and you know what you want, let's get into the practical aspects of winning big accounts.

## Critical Points from This Chapter

- Most of us make the mistake of focusing only on a company's end product when considering our market potential with the company. We assume a company that makes widgets is only interested in suppliers who can make widget parts.
- Not a single experienced buyer we surveyed picked the lowest-priced vendor, and the reason they gave for choosing the higher-priced vendor was either (a) "history of delivery" or (b) "quality standards of the vendor."
- A delivery problem is virtually always the reason you will lose a sale to one of your existing customers.
- The absolute best suppliers work closely with their clients to ensure that delivery of needed goods and services is just-in-time (JIT). It may be exactly this kind of responsiveness that your giant accounts require, so don't be unprepared.
- Many domestic corporations go beyond U.S. borders to find qualified suppliers. Why? Because there is unfortunately a widely held perception that domestic suppliers can't meet the quality standards that large corporations seek.
- Quality doesn't always literally mean "best." A quality product or service is one that conforms to your customer's

*(continued)*

*(continued)*

standards and expectations. Quality means the right stuff, not necessarily the best stuff.

- If your goal is to serve as a key supplier to a giant corporation or government entity, your mission should be clear: Make the purchasing agent or executive's job easier.

- If you're going to sell to the giants, you need to be diligent about setting realistic but challenging goals for yourself—and holding yourself accountable for following through. Only being "planful" will get you where you want to be.

# Finding Friendly Giants

N ow that you've set some specific goals for winning new contracts with giant corporations and government agencies, you need to take action! The good news is that finding friendly giants is actually far easier than you think. As noted in the first chapter, many organizations have specific mandates to use small business suppliers and have established programs for working with small businesses. Companies like these do everything they can to make information available to businesses like ours, ensuring that we have equal opportunities to bid on contracts and propose projects to them. Although not all of your prospects are going to lay out the red carpet for you, there are ways to increase your odds of winning their business.

## Friendly Giants Are Out There

Most major corporations have good intentions when it comes to awarding contracts to new suppliers. In fact, many firms have modified procurement procedures to be more responsive to smaller business suppliers.

- Some corporations predetermine which contracts will be limited to small and small minority-owned businesses. In this way, there is ample time to outline qualifications and specifications for the small suppliers months in advance.
- Some contracts are earmarked to be sole-source, nonbid proposals, competitive bids for small business vendors, or both. From their list of eligible suppliers, some corporations develop a list of qualified suppliers for each contract—well before contract announcement or proposal solicitation, so that less time is wasted qualifying eligible suppliers. Job size has a lot to do with this determination, along with knowledge of capable suppliers with whom the purchasing department is already acquainted.

- Some firms cut down the number of unqualified proposals submitted by providing small suppliers with a checklist of what they need and don't need to qualify for specific contracts. (The largest portion of time in the procurement cycle is spent determining whether a group of small suppliers actually qualifies to perform a particular job.) Also, in recent years procurement processing time has been cut by streamlining forms and other documentation required from small business suppliers.

- Some corporations set priorities for small business procurement by establishing time frames for job announcements, bid or proposal deadlines, and contract award announcements.

- Many corporations are striving for better communication with small vendors. Better communication means that less time is required to convey contract needs and there are fewer misunderstandings that lead to delays in the procurement process. Progressive corporations have designated a procurement spokesperson to deal with small vendors exclusively, usually titled something like "small business coordinator." With a single representative communicating with the suppliers, inappropriate, unneeded, and time-consuming communications between the wrong parties are eliminated.

- Increasingly, corporations are providing all contract information and specifications in one package to avoid costly revisions and time delays for the suppliers.

- Some corporations advise small businesses as soon as possible when their proposals or bids fail to meet qualification standards. This policy gives you a chance to move on and concentrate on another opportunity, having learned something useful that will strengthen your position. Also when you've been informed of why you didn't receive a contract award in timely fashion, you'll tend to think more highly of responding to that corporation in the future. If the company doesn't volunteer this information, ask. You may not get an answer, but if you do, the information you receive can be invaluable in helping you avoid mistakes and present your firm's capabilities more effectively in the future.

- Many large corporations and government agencies participate in initiatives like business matchmaking (BMM) events, which support procurement opportunities for small business. BMM, SCORE® Counselors to America's Small Business and others have online portals that can be very useful to small businesses.

## Navigating the Corporate Maze

We hear stories all the time about challenges salespeople and business development executives face just getting in front of decision makers. In fact, a small business owner named Robert was just telling me about reading his morning news feed and noticing a particularly interesting item: A multinational firm headquartered in the next county was announcing an expansion of its product line to include hydraulic brakes. Robert owns and manages a firm that produces components used in these brake assemblies, so he immediately saw a potentially large new customer for his components. He called the company's corporate headquarters to speak with the purchasing department. The receptionist informed him that no purchasing personnel are located at the firm's headquarters. Robert then asked for the correct number to call and waited on hold while the receptionist checked. After several minutes, the receptionist finally returned with the name of an East Coast plant where purchasing activities took place and gave Robert the number.

Robert had to be tenacious. He called the East Coast location and received help from the receptionist there to identify the correct purchasing manager for the new hydraulic brake product line. Success at last, and he was connected to the proper office—only to be told that the purchasing manager he needed circulates around the region and would be in Tennessee for three weeks. Robert got the Tennessee plant's telephone number and placed his third long-distance call. He located the purchasing manager—amazingly—and began introducing himself and his product to her.

Robert got a few sentences in, only to have the purchasing manager politely inform him that she was not, in fact, the right person to talk with, and that he should contact someone else. This all probably sounds painfully familiar to you. Navigating the corporate maze can feel like herding cats, and it's not really surprising, given that people within large corporations sometimes even have trouble finding one another.

Once you have determined which large corporations and government agencies you'd like to do business with, there are steps you can take to find out whether the firms are small business–friendly and make the process of locating and contacting key decision makers easier. "Fishing" attempts by telephone, like Robert's, are almost always unproductive. Robert had the right idea to follow up on a decent sales lead, but he chose the wrong way to do it. Here are four simple methods for beginning to navigate the corporate maze:

1. **Seek Supplier Guides.** Many corporations post supplier guides on their Web sites. If not, call or e-mail the company's purchasing department to receive copies of any supplier guides, supplier application forms, and a list of products purchased.

2. **Ask for Corporate News.** Most companies' Web sites are chock-full of valuable information and corporate publications. If not, write to the public relations office for copies of the company's newsletter, in-house publications, and any recent press releases on what the company is doing. These services may contain useful information that can help you tailor your sales approach. It's not likely that you'll be put on the company's mailing list, but the sample(s) you do receive will certainly give you a sense of how the company operates and some of the things it values.

3. **Contact the Small Business Liaison Office.** Contact the small business coordinator by phone or e-mail, explaining your product or service and your interest in becoming a supplier to the corporation. Raytheon, Dow Corning, Owens-Illinois, and 3M, among hundreds of others, provide names and phone numbers of plants and purchasing agents. Not all firms have a coordinator; nevertheless, you will receive a response indicating the name, title, and location of a person who can handle your request.

4. **Contact a Top Executive.** Giant corporations typically have countless locations that are fairly autonomous, and getting through to a decision maker at a division or facility level is much easier than trying for the corporate CEO. In most cases, division-level executives have decision-making authority (and as we've already discussed, winning business at the division level may be a more realistic goal for a small business, at least initially).

## Learning from Supplier Guides

The friendliest giants make well written, informative supplier guides available to small businesses from their corporate Web sites or on request from their purchasing department. In most cases, these guides include information about products and services purchased, corporate policies and purchasing procedures, purchasing/supply chain contact names and numbers, and supplier registration forms that will prequalify your firm for doing business with the corporation. Corporations everywhere are recognizing that such a guide is essential for developing mutually beneficial relations that extend far beyond the simple process of buying and selling.

Sometimes, after reviewing a supplier guide, you may decide that you do not have the products or services that are in need. Thus, you have saved yourself valuable time you might have otherwise spent navigating the corporate maze to no avail. But if you do decide to move ahead, the guide will familiarize you with various corporate policies and procedures so that you can give a better presentation to the appropriate people once you've discovered what requirement(s) you can fulfill.

I know all too well that supplier registration or application forms seem like a pointless corporate delaying tactic. In truth, though, they are a critical step in becoming a supplier to the giants, and you should fill them out as completely and accurately as possible. Many corporations, such as Philip Morris and McDonnell Douglas, use the information on these forms to produce directories of potential suppliers, which then are distributed to buyers throughout their respective corporations. These directories serve as "ready references" when a new source or new materials are required, and inclusion in them signifies to buyers that your firm has been vetted and approved, reducing buyers' fears of the unknown and ensuring that their buying decisions are consistent with corporate requirements.

When you look at the supplier registration or application form, you may feel a little overwhelmed, but there is no advantage in beefing up your credentials on application forms. I've seen small suppliers who added 50 percent to their plant's square footage, "doubled" their number of employees, and added several years to how long they've been in business. Your best chance is to maintain 100 percent honesty—really. It will serve you better in the short run, because most purchasing agents have seen it all already, and it won't help you be taken seriously. And in the long run, if you've fibbed or exaggerated a claim, you'll likely be found out, which will cost you in credibility.

## Why Should We Buy from You?

It's worth repeating that winning business from the giants takes work—and a lot of it. Before you ever get the opportunity to bid on a particular project or be listed in an approved suppliers directory, you have to demonstrate to the corporation or agency that you're worth it. In the initial stages of seeking to engage large corporations or government entities (just as with any other sales opportunity), you'll find that one question is at the forefront: Why should we buy from you? Large companies have access to almost limitless providers and suppliers, so your goal should be defining and articulating what distinguishes your company and your products/services from your competitors'.

For the most part, this isn't really any different from when you're selling to smaller firms, is it? Selling to anyone requires differentiating yourself, your product/service, and your company in your prospect's mind. The primary difference I see is that giant organizations tend to have more stringent, stated requirements for quality and delivery, and they have more "standardized" systems for payment terms, underperformance/error penalties, and so on.

One supplier's guide I saw recently presented the following questionnaire as a checklist for vendors, and it's by no means the longest or most comprehensive questionnaire I've seen.

1. Have you presented a new idea to us lately?
2. What is your best idea to reduce our cost?
3. Do you have products or services that will increase our productivity? How?
4. Will your organization provide technical services to us? Are your complete capabilities known to us? Are we using them?
5. Do you tell us promptly of new products or new ways to use existing ones?
6. What is your approach to quality? Do you know the consistency of the product you ship us—or just think you do—or assume it is OK unless you receive complaints?
7. What are you doing to improve consistency of your product quality?
8. Are you willing to certify your shipments to us as meeting quality standards?

9. Have you established a record of "delivery reliability" with us? Is every shipment of your product within agreed-to tolerances, properly packaged and marked with code number, with the exact count, and shipped to the proper destination?

10. Do you always ship only the quantity ordered? (No overage unless within the agreed-to size.)

11. Do you always ship on the specified date—and not before, unless the purchase order permits early shipment? Do you always ship as instructed by us?

12. What specific ideas can you offer to minimize transportation costs on items we buy from you?

13. Will you hold prices longer for more business? Terms are a part of price. We pay on time. Are your quoted prices on the basis of our prompt payment?

14. Have you developed a "Volume Discount" program with us?

15. Do you participate in our "Committed Stock" program?

16. Are you interested in consignment inventory on or near our premises? Vendor stocking, on your premises, may offer opportunities for additional volume.

17. Review your lead time requirements with us. Shorter lead times may give you a competitive advantage.


You can see that this giant is willing to reward strong performance and supplier effort and initiative with loyalty and volume. It's also obvious from the list that this particular large company has very clear expectations of its vendors, and it has put effort into standardizing requirements and reducing costs wherever possible. Remember, though, that cost reduction isn't always correlated with lowest price.

You should instead be concentrating on the value that you offer the giant, with reasonable price being only part of that equation. The giants are interested not just in buying a product or a service—a valve or a training program. They're interested in partnering with small businesses who will treat the giants' business with the dedication to creativity and commitment to quality they'd have in their own firms.

# Before You Pick Up the Phone or Complete Supplier Qualification Forms

As you can see, corporations want to ensure that the small businesses they select as suppliers can meet their requirements and serve them as effectively as larger organizations can. To make the most of the prequalification process, I strongly advise you to do your research about your prospect. Being thorough may give you the edge you need to stand out in a crowded marketplace filled with qualified providers/suppliers.

## Six Essential Elements of Profiling an Organization

Gathering information on the following six essential elements will provide a brief but effective corporation profile. This type of profile affords quick review, updating, and use for sales calls.

1.  **Operations**—an overview of what the company does, including major markets, number of plants, total personnel, and other pertinent information.
2.  **Sales**—sales of the corporation as reflected in its most recent annual report and its ranking within its industry based on lists in *Forbes* or *Fortune*.
3.  **Outlook**—where the corporation is heading, new product and service areas, significant management initiatives, and other information that indicates the direction of the corporation.
4.  **Product and Services**—an in-depth list of the company's products or services.

5. **Tips for Suppliers**—information on vendor and small vendor utilization programs, purchasing structure and procedures, specialized buying needs that you may be able to fulfill, and strategy hints for contacting and marketing to the corporation.

6. **Contact**—name and phone number of the person(s) with responsibility for facilitating supplier marketing efforts within the corporation. If applicable, includes names and phone numbers of divisional purchasing contacts.

There are many additional ways to gain vital data and information about corporate targets; most are a few clicks away on the Internet or a quick visit to your local library. Reference librarians can help you access publications you may not have known about, and many libraries have subscriptions to resources like Hoover's, which you can use for free if you're at the library. The more you can narrow your search, the better. And the more you know about the company you're calling on and the trends in their industry, even better.

## Use Annual Reports and 10k Reports

Call or write to the company's shareholder information office and ask for a copy of the annual report. There is a wealth of information in most annual reports!

### The CEO's report may include details about:

- Expansion plans
- Warning of "streamlining" operations (may indicate closing of some facilities)
- New social responsibility or awareness programs
- New product lines
- Diversification

**Consolidated income statements likely give you information about:**

- Tracking net revenue over time
- Tracking percentage change over time
- Observed increases or decreases

**An auditor's letter will reveal:**

- Exceptions or notes to financial statements
- Any "one-time" accounting entries
- Changes in accounting methods

## Make the Most of Professional and Trade Associations

A professional or trade association exists for every industry and type of business. Most associations maintain a membership directory that can provide a ready-made target list for you. Association directories can be found online and in any library and offer the names, addresses, and phone numbers of your industry's trade and professional associations. A few we've used:

- www.associationsdirectory.org
- Gale's Encyclopedia of Associations
- National Trade and Professional Associations (NTPA) Directory

Some associations administer a professional referral system, whereby key individuals with specific expertise within the industry may be identified. Using an association referral system for industries that require high technology or highly specialized suppliers is an excellent way to become less "hard to find."

## Consult Databases and Newspaper Indexes

If you want to find an article or information on a corporation that appeared in your local newspaper, often your public library will contain a newspaper index that abstracts newspaper articles by topic and cross-references this listing by date. Your metro area may also be served by one or more area business publications. You can write to the Association of Area Business Publications' Web site at www.bizpubs.org for a complete city-by-city list.

**A few other places to look for information:**
- The *Wall Street Journal Index*
- Gebbie Press *All-in-One Media Directory*
- *Bacon's Publicity Checker*
- *Standard Periodicals Directory*
- *Standard and Poor's Register*
- *Thomas Register of American Manufacturers*
- *Dun and Bradstreet's Million Dollar Directory*
- *Hoover's*
- Supplier guides, often called blue books or red books, can be found in the business reference section of many public libraries. For example, the "Blue Book of Metro Area Home Builders," and the "Red Book of Plumbing Supply Contractors," are often issued by the local associations serving these industries.

## Ask Uncle Sam for Help

The federal government is one of the largest publishers in the world. Through the Bureau of Census of the Department of Commerce, you may obtain sales and revenue data on virtually any industry, by state, county, and standard metropolitan statistical area. Although the Bureau of Census is primarily known for its population reports, a census of business is taken on the second and seventh year of each decade and is generally available 18 months thereafter.

Census information is provided on industries, businesses, and products according to the North American Industry Classification System (NAICS), which replaced the Standard Industrial Classification (SIC) system of codes. Census data are collected for thousands of material categories and quantity and product classifications, and this information is compiled by NAICS codes. Separate censuses are conducted for manufacturers, mineral industries, construction industries, retail trade, wholesale trade, and service industries, so you'll be able to find a wealth of detail in virtually any category you'd like to investigate.

The Department of Commerce annually publishes the *U.S. Industrial Outlook*, which traces the growth of 200 industries and provides five-year forecasts for each industry. The U.S. Statistical Abstract is a compilation of data and reports from the Department of Commerce, the Department of Labor, the Department of Transportation, the Small Business Administration, and other federal agencies.

## State and Local Information Sources

All 50 U.S. states have their own Department of Commerce, and nearly all have special offices established to assist small or disadvantaged businesses. The state capitol and state capitol library, the governor's office, as well as the offices of your elected officials, often maintain special reports, studies, and analysis that may prove useful in your marketing research efforts.

On a regional or local basis, various planning communities, the research department of newspapers, highway commissions, local libraries, and the county courthouse are just a few of the information sources you may wish to tap, depending on your research need. Many entrepreneurs have found that a wealth of information can be gained right over the phone or by simply visiting nearby organizations or agencies.

The local Chamber of Commerce has figures for the types of business in your area and estimation of profits, number of new people moving into the area, listings of local media, and so on. At both the local and national levels, it is a valuable source of information. Local colleges and universities can also be a useful source of information on the size and accessibility of your market. These institutions can sometimes offer assistance or advice through graduate research programs.

## How to Find Information about Government Prospects

The federal government, as well as your state and local governments, can be a huge source of potential business for you, regardless of what you sell. There's enough information about this topic to fill another book, but let me give you a few Web sites and other resources to get you started:

- FedBizOpps.gov—the place to search and monitor all opportunities posted by the federal government.
- Small Business Administration—if you want to sell to the government, you first have to understand how the contracting process works, determine whether your business qualifies, and decide whether government contracting is right for you. The SBA is a great place to start.
- GSA Advantage—The GSA identifies potential vendors, awards contracts, and helps ensure federal contracting regulations and requirements are met. GSA connects the public sector with industry experts through GSAAdvantage.gov and simplifies the contracting process to save agencies time and money. Vendors and suppliers can register on the Web site to get information about how to market to government agencies.

Most states have Web sites that list government business opportunities; I strongly recommend that you locate the site for your state. Don't overlook your local government either. Most source products and services locally to keep money in the region.

## Golden Rules

A primary golden rule for becoming a key supplier to corporate giants is to *join associations*, such as the groups described earlier, composed of purchasing agents and of other vendors. If you get no other benefit, your membership status will help mark your business as one of distinction.

The *ability to be flexible* is an essential element to successfully compete in our dynamic technologically driven society. Rapid change has a profound effect on individuals and their ability to keep pace in society. Such change creates an ever-increasing array of opportunities for bold, innovative entrepreneurs.

One of the fastest ways to accelerate the rate at which you penetrate a corporate giant is to *identify the 10 people whom you must know and meet them.* These 10 key contacts are different for everyone, but generally include the head of your industry's association, the director of key publications in your field, directors of the corporation, key purchasing agents at the target corporation, a Small Business Administration management assistance officer, the small business liaison, operations or facilities managers, and assorted others based on the specifics of your product or service offering.

Having identified the 10 people that you must know, the next step is to meet them. Write to them, call them, go to their office, and go to the conventions they attend. Your goal is to make sure that they know who you are and what goods and services you provide.

Particularly if you are *known for something*—providing superior service, being the best producer of your product in the world, for example—make sure they know it. The key 10 with whom you make contact will have an easier time remembering you and your company and what you stand for. What do you want to be known for?

**Tie short-run objectives to long-run goals.** When you take on new tasks, do you carefully assess what is the downstream potential? Are you forced to take on new jobs to pay the bills? Or do you carefully assess a contract's potential for maintaining your working capital requirements and adding to the experience, track record, and capabilities of your company?

**Look for opportunities in adversity.** The notion of looking for opportunities in adversity may sound to some like a platitude. It's not. Those who accept adversity as defeat are defeated. Those who see adversity as a normal occurrence within the life of a business survive. And those who view adversity as the flip side of opportunity succeed. This is a prime example of why it's a good idea to learn why you didn't win a contract—there's tremendous opportunity in learning from your mistakes and failures.

**Simplify! Simplify!** Henry David Thoreau said it well and said it best over 150 years ago. Our lives and our businesses are "simply cluttered" with too many activities, and too many slips of paper, that simply don't support us.

**Learn from your experiences.** Learn from what went wrong and what went right, but invest in the future. You and your company are not just an extension of what came before today, because you have the ability to create. What products or services do you want to be offering a year from now? Three years from now? What profit level do you want to realize on the contracts you undertake? What do you want your image to be in the marketplace?

If you view your business and your sales and marketing efforts as being inexorably tied to what came before, then all you have ever been is all you will ever be. How does the supplier who has never landed a contract with a corporate giant finally get one? Or examining the larger question: How do losers ever win? By going where they have never gone before. By doing what they fear. By doing what winners do.

## Critical Points from This Chapter

- Many organizations have specific mandates to use small business suppliers and have established programs for working with small businesses. Companies like these do everything they can to make information available to businesses like ours, ensuring that we have equal opportunities to bid on contracts and propose projects to them.

- Here are four simple methods for beginning to navigate the corporate maze:

  1. Seek supplier guides.

  2. Ask for corporate news.

  3. Contact the small business liaison office.

  4. Contact a top executive.

- Supplier registration or application forms may seem like a pointless corporate delaying tactic. In truth, though, they are a critical step in becoming a supplier to the giants, and you should fill them out as completely and accurately as possible.

- Being thorough in your pre-call planning efforts may give you the edge you need to stand out in a crowded marketplace filled with qualified providers/suppliers.

- One of the fastest ways to accelerate the rate at which you penetrate corporate giants is to identify the people you must know and meet them. Generally, this includes the head of your industry's association, the director/editor of key publications in your field, a banker, a few directors of your target corporation(s), key purchasing agents, and so on.

- If you view your business and sales and marketing efforts as being inexorably tied to what came before, then all you have ever been is all you will ever be.

# How Corporations Buy

**Supply Management:** The identification, acquisition, access, positioning and management of resources and related capabilities the organization needs or potentially needs in the attainment of its strategic objectives. (Institute for Supply Management)

## Variety in Purchasing Procedures

The corporations we sell to have all kinds of purchasing programs and methods of buying. We won one of our largest clients by responding to a detailed request for proposal (RFP) issued through the company's purchasing department, and business we earned from another giant was the direct result of my meeting with a VP-level employee of the firm. On the surface, almost everything about the two contracts is different—from how we interface with the company's personnel to how we submit invoices to how we propose new projects to them.

However, there's one key factor that our relationship with these two clients has in common: decision makers at our clients' organizations see us as a strategic partner, not merely a provider of a single service or product. In fact, our ability to serve as a strategic partner was a significant factor in both clients' decision to outsource sales and sales management training and assessment services to us. Our ongoing, day-to-day collaboration with each client means that we're in the best possible position to serve our clients' current and future requirements. Again, we're not merely providing a single service or product—we're integrated into the very fabric of each organization's sales and marketing effort.

As I said, we took two quite different routes to earn business from two very different giant organizations. You've no doubt observed the same thing in your sales career: What works for selling to one client may not work at all for another. Because corporations have so many different procedures for soliciting bids and awarding contracts, it's easy to get overwhelmed by the thought of trying to pursue giant organizations because you're not sure where to start. In this chapter, I'm going to try to give you an overview of how corporations—in general—make purchases. Although each company does buy differently, I can at least give you some pointers on where to start and how the purchasing function operates in most large companies and government organizations.

## Purchasing and the Supply Chain

We're in the midst of a major shift in how corporations approach the idea of purchasing. Exactly what is changing? Here's a hint: In 2001, the organization that was known as the National Association of Purchasing Management changed its name to the Institute for Supply Management. In the past, purchasing was simply that—purchasing. Purchasing department personnel were told what was needed and tasked with finding sources of the necessary goods or services at the best prices. But by the early 1990s, the purchasing function at modern firms gained stature, taking on such strategic missions as sourcing to seek savings, looking globally for solutions, planning material inventories and flow, and even playing a key role in new product development.

Obviously, today's purchasing department isn't just about buying things on request. You'll find that many departments that used to be called "Purchasing" are now called things like "Supply Management" or "Sourcing"—titles that signify the greater strategic role the function plays in the organization. In truth, procurement efforts have become essential to companies' value propositions. Think about it: If your firm can do a better job of getting your product delivered to the end user, when they want it, and at a better price than your competitors, you're eons ahead. How do you accomplish these goals? Careful sourcing of raw materials that go into making your product, efficient processing and manufacturing of your product (or development of your service), smart inventory management, and flawless order management—all are functions of supply management.

This is the basic background for selling to giant corporations and government agencies: you need to be prepared to navigate the maze of a purchasing department that seeks to ensure that corporate missions are achieved with the effective, timely, and fairly priced assistance of a select group of preferred suppliers, like your company. Purchasing department personnel are typically well educated, market savvy, and knowledgeable about the products and services they are tasked with sourcing and acquiring.

## Essential Performance Factors

Major corporations choose their vendors and suppliers with care to achieve a good "fit" in products and processes. Life of the program contracts and corporate-sponsored vendor training are just two indicators of how critical supplier dependability is to the largest companies. Purchasers at giant corporations and government agencies alike are tasked with sourcing products and services that meet strict guidelines; if your company can meet these requirements, they'll be willing to invest effort and resources into your endeavor to ensure a long-term, profitable partnership. And "partnership" is the key word here. Most modern purchasing organizations look at their suppliers as strategic partners, not just providers of goods.

However, although corporate purchasers will want to see that you understand the strategic implications of the work you're doing for them, supplier *performance*—the tactical, day-to-day activity—is the responsibility of the purchasing department at most 21st century corporations. In the past, cost reduction may have been the overriding concern for many corporate purchasing managers, but no longer. At an annual conference of the Institute for Supply Management, this message came through loud and clear. One speaker, a vice president for a leading international telecommunications corporation, said, "If you don't demand the best from your suppliers, your company won't end up with the best product."

**Key performance factors that separate the best from the rest include:**

- quality of purchased items,
- lead times,
- communication between supplier and buyer, and
- supplier representatives' level of knowledge and technical expertise.

As discussed in Chapter 2, of these factors, *demonstrated* quality and reliability are by far the most important.

To select from many potential suppliers, corporate purchasing personnel—who work in departments called purchasing, procurement, and supply chain management—typically follow a comprehensive procedure for soliciting input, evaluating suppliers against the ideal and one another, and awarding contracts for specific pieces of business. In many cases, corporate and government purchasing offices prequalify a group of vendors, who are then asked to bid against one another on specific projects.

Naturally, buyers may attempt to negotiate with a short list of preferred suppliers for better prices and terms before making their final selection. In the end, they may select a single supplier or a few suppliers. Many buyers prefer multiple sources of supply so that they will not be totally dependent on one supplier in case something goes wrong and they will be able to compare the prices and performance of the various suppliers. This is especially true of companies that sell things like critical equipment, replacement parts, and other products that must have 100 percent uptime.

This isn't true for just product providers, it's also true for service providers. At The Brooks Group, we sell training, assessments, and other sales-related products and often provide complete sales and sales management programs for our clients. But in one significant case, we provide large volumes of assessments for hiring, training, and management for our client; but the client uses another sales training firm for its sales training needs. The company had an existing, positive relationship with one of our competitors, but it didn't stop them from using us where they felt we could make the most impact. Obviously, our goal is that in the future, The Brooks Group will earn the sales training aspect of business from the client, too. The point is that just because you know a competitor has an existing relationship with a prospective client doesn't mean the client won't have interest in what you have to offer.

## Typical Procedures

Procurement processes and cycles differ from company to company—and sometimes within divisions of a company—but most large corporations:

- **Have some variety of vendor prequalification process.** Many firms make this process easy to begin by posting all guidelines and application forms online—large companies like Volvo and Bank of America have comprehensive potential supplier guides easily accessible on their Web sites, and many government agencies like the U.S. Air Force do as well.

- **Require that suppliers be able to meet stringent requirements in the areas of quality, delivery, safety, and price.** Particularly in manufacturing, suppliers may be required to meet the most current lean process standards or other quality, safety, and environmental regulations. Remember, don't get hung up on "price," meaning the cheapest price. Just like everyone else, the giants are looking for prices they can justify—fair prices for the valuable products or services you sell.

- **Publish a list of prequalified vendors to division and branch personnel.** Once you've passed the initial prequalification process, you'll be included in a preferred provider list. This will "fast track" your firm, so you'll receive notifications of RFPs and direct contacts from plant and/or facility purchasing personnel who want to buy what you sell.

- **Develop detailed RFPs or requests for quote (RFQs) for projects over a certain dollar value or scope.** Once you're considered a preferred provider/supplier, you—and other preferred providers—will be eligible to submit responses to these requests. These RFPs and RFQs will give you specific instructions for describing the product or service you offer and for pricing it in appropriate quantities.

- **Make "team" decisions about potential major suppliers.** In most large organizations, a committee of personnel review RFP responses and make collaborative decisions about contract awards. You may be asked to make a presentation to this team or field questions from individual members of the team.

- **Develop detailed, specific contracts that protect their interests and describe what role(s) your firm and theirs will perform.** This is an essential part of doing business with large corporations and one that smaller suppliers often underestimate. Contract negotiations can be long and difficult. (We'll look more at this phase of the sale in Chapter 10.)

- **Make full use of online technologies to manage the sourcing and buying process.** Advances in technology enable virtual management of enormous supplier networks—the most sophisticated large corporations manage all aspects of buying from trusted suppliers electronically, with no paper exchanged at any point in the solicitation-purchase-payment timeline.

As I said, each company has its own procedures and policies for purchasing goods and services, so specific details will vary depending on the company. The best first step you can take is to get in touch with the purchasing—or supply management—department of the corporation you're interested in and explain that you'd like to learn more about becoming a supplier. Before you make that call, though, let's look at how purchasing departments are typically organized and whom you should be prepared to interface with.

## Understanding the Purchasing Department

In some large companies, all purchases must be routed through the Purchasing or Supply Management Department, whereas in others, management-level employees in all departments have purchasing authority up to a predetermined dollar amount. There are three basic categories into which purchasing departments can be organized. Of course, there are variations on each of these types, but in general, these categories are useful:

- **Centralized.** One large purchasing department at corporate headquarters makes all buying decisions for every plant and facility within the corporation.
- **Semicentralized.** The headquarters' purchasing department typically purchases all big-ticket items for the corporation, and plant or branch purchasing personnel acquire their own small or specialized items. Purchases by individual facilities may be limited by total dollars spent, with approval needed from headquarters for any amount over the limit.
- **Decentralized.** Each plant or facility purchases all of its materials, equipment, and services. A headquarters purchasing department may oversee individual locations, but the amount of the influence they have varies with each corporation.

Today most companies have a decentralized or semicentralized purchasing organization. Amazing levels of collaboration and cooperation have been made possible by the Internet and associated Web-based applications such as project management software, real-time inventory management systems, customer relationship management systems, and so on. Just be sure you know what's common in the industries into which you sell, and be able to integrate your systems to the industry standard applications.

## Your First Point of Contact

Do your research up front; if the corporation has a small business supplier coordinator, consider this person your first and most important contact. To ignore their important advice and assistance can significantly decrease your sales effectiveness, because it is the responsibility of the coordinator to ensure that suppliers like you have all the information they need to make a credible attempt at becoming a preferred supplier. I am often pleasantly surprised at the assistance provided by corporations' small vendor coordinators, who don't just provide background information and details about corporate buying procedures, but also can help you gain access to key engineering and technical personnel.

If your prospect doesn't have a small business supplier coordinator, you have two other good options: (a) the top-most executive in charge of the business unit you're attempting to sell into and (b) the purchasing manager for the product or service you sell. If the corporation is decentralized, as a majority are, make an appointment with the appropriate plant or facility purchasing manager or buyer. Even if purchasing personnel are not technically oriented themselves, they will be able to help you identify needs within the corporation. And purchasing will have the final say regardless of what connections you make with the technical staff (in fact, they can make things difficult for a supplier they feel is attempting an "end-run").

Alternatively—and I usually prefer this option—start as high as you can go. Executives have the best view into the company or business unit's strategic plans and usually have the authority to make buying decisions. If worst comes to worst, the executive (or his or her assistant) will lead you to the purchasing manager, and you've lost nothing.

## Contacting Technical Staff or Project Team Leaders

Does it help to make your capabilities known to others not in purchasing? In a word: yes. The director of administration services at one large transportation agency is responsible for writing and establishing supply specifications. Although he has no actual purchasing authority, he frequently receives brochures and capability statements from prospective suppliers. "I pass along everything I get to the appropriate purchasing people," he says. "However, I do read what suppliers send in, and if I happen to come across a particularly attractive package from a seemingly high qualified supplier, I let purchasing know."

There are ways to find out the technical needs of a corporation without directly asking or bypassing the purchasing department. Join appropriate local associations of engineers or other professionals and listen to their discussions. When you contact the purchasing department, you can say that you heard about a certain technical need through a social contact and you would like some advice on the proper channels to follow.

Another way to find out the specific needs of a corporation is to ask the purchasing staff member for an appointment to see the specifying engineer. This person is responsible for specific materials used on a job and will often recommend to the purchasing department that a certain supplier be used. Particularly in high-technology areas especially, such "preselections" are often made very early in the procurement process. The specifying engineer may even be assigned to the purchasing department. Asking to see him will show your interest in the project and, again, your willingness to work with the purchasing department "through the proper channels."

"Suppliers who take the initiative to analyze and evaluate needs and functions can uncover many opportunities for good payback," reported one manager of procurement with an aircraft manufacturing company. Corporations appreciate, and often count on, the input of suppliers for value engineering savings. If you can find the names of the key team members for a particular project before you see the purchasing department, you will make a favorable impression for having done your homework and perhaps gain key inside information. You might wish to call the switchboard and ask in advance for the name of the leader on a specific project, but not actually speak to him or her until you have checked with the purchasing department.

### Play Both against the Middle

Purchasing, technical personnel, and company executives are complementary in function. As a supplier, you must satisfy the requirements of all to be prosperous. Use purchasing to identify general needs and to make appointments with the appropriate technical people. Impress the technical department with your capabilities and understanding of their needs. If you can demonstrate that you recognize the importance and function of each department, you may well end up with both departments on your side. And if you can get the executive level to see the positive impact your product or service can have on multiple business fronts, you've really positioned yourself and your offering effectively.

## Vendor Prequalification

Corporate buyers today need a great deal of information before choosing a company for a prime supplier. Corporate purchasing agents are expecting more from their suppliers, particularly in the area of quality. Some companies estimate that they purchase

70 percent of their quality problems; the vast majority of end-product quality headaches are shipped into their plants by suppliers in the form of subpar purchased goods and materials. One purchasing agent observed, "there is no way we can improve the quality of what we are doing" without improvements in incoming components.

## Few(er) Are Chosen

Back in the 1980s, the Xerox Corporation undertook a "drastic pruning" of its supplier base while providing intensive training to key suppliers in statistical process control and just-in-time inventory systems. Xerox continues to help suppliers with personal development programs and longer-term contracts that compel suppliers "to become business partners, and build confidence to the point where suppliers share what they have learned."

Xerox was at the forefront of a major change in how industrial corporations buy the goods and services they need. At virtually all industrial corporations, the average number of suppliers has significantly declined, whereas single sourcing (finding the source of supply for a particular item or service) has grown in popularity. More than ever, observes one veteran, relationships are up for grabs. "Even long-standing personal relationships are at risk." Some purchasers are limiting the number of sales representatives who call on them.

When a corporate giant makes the decision to reduce their supplier base, it enables that corporation to maintain more direct and effective communications with the remaining suppliers and at the same time increases corporate leverage over those suppliers, because each supplier does more business with the corporate giant and thus is more dependent on the corporate giant. The net result for you is clear.

If you want to achieve favored vendor or supplier status among corporations who have been tearing down their supplier base, you will have to understand and serve their needs more than ever before and position your company to become the type of supplier purchasing agents want to call on—the focus of this book.

## Getting Qualified

The point of a corporation's vendor/supplier prequalification process is for you to document your company's ability to provide products or services that have practicality and value for the corporation. In most cases, you may seek to become prequalified at any time during the company's fiscal year. As soon as you receive approved bidder status, you'll be notified of projects for which the company wishes you to provide solutions. In the prequalification phase of the sale, the purchasing agent with whom you will deal will be keenly interested in your capabilities regarding the big three: price, quality, and delivery. Agents will require considerable documentation relating to your firm's history, track record, and capabilities. In the following sections, you'll find a description of typical details you'll be asked to provide in the prequalification process.

## Ownership

A description of ownership is generally the first item in your capability statement. How is your business organized? The purchasing agent or buyer will want to know whether your firm is a sole proprietorship, partnership, or corporation. If your business is a corporation, list the members of your board of directors and the stockholders, including their respective ownership percentages. If you are a sole proprietorship or a partnership, list the members of your advisory board. Incidentally, if you don't have an advisory board, consider creating one using experienced businesspeople, retired bankers, and college professors with specialties in your field and seek their advice.

If you are a minority- or woman-owned business, say so and elaborate on the percentage of ownership. Be sure to mention if your business is certified as a minority-owned firm by federal, state, or local agencies, or by any other organization (e.g., a public utility). Many corporations have supplier diversity programs that ensure specific levels of minority- and women-owned suppliers and service providers.

## Market Served

Specify which market you are attempting to serve and why your products/services meet the needs of this market. Many entrepreneurs and salespeople fluctuate almost daily, making half-hearted attempts to penetrate first one market, then a second, and then a third. They never stop to decide which market they should penetrate first. The quixotic approach simply doesn't work.

An important step in effective prospecting is setting aside time to learn about the operating characteristics of the industry and businesses to whom you wish to sell. What from your past experience can be drawn on and used as a competitive advantage in penetrating your chosen market? What do you currently offer that is consistent with the changing needs of the market?

A product or service that fulfills the needs of a specifically defined group is preferable to one that compromises to suit widely divergent needs. By targeting a particular segment, you can tailor your product to more closely serve your customer's needs. The closer the match, the greater the potential for sales. Descriptive terminology in this section might encompass geographic area and climate, terrain, natural resources, population density, cultural values; the usage rate for the product-heavy, moderate, or light; the type of organization; customer size; and use of the product.

For example, one company's market for sale of uniforms consists of corporations, hospitals, laboratories, police departments, fire departments, fast food chains, grocery store chains, municipal workers (e.g., sanitation workers, road crews), and prisons in a 200-mile radius of its mill.

## Products/Services

Your firm's products or services should be clearly and completely described, and all of your firm's locations, including addresses and phone numbers, should be listed, including the one at which you can be most readily found. Are you innovative in your approach to product/service offerings? Innovative means providing better and more economical goods and services than your competitors. Suppliers to the giants must be prepared to be involved in a collaborative effort, often starting from the design level.

If you can, identify features of your product or service that distinguish it and make your firm stand out from the others. Here are a few quick examples:

Comprehensive service program
Better product, even at a higher price
New uses for existing products/services
New distribution methods

New production methods
New marketing techniques
Lower prices
On-site services

Greater durability
Portability and ease of use

Guarantees beyond industry norms
Extended product life/parts availability
"Green" features/benefits
Training programs
Safety guarantees
24/7 technical support

## Recent Successful Projects and Activities

A concise description of recent projects on which your firm has performed well should be included in this section. If you have references or testimonial letters commending your firm and the job you have done, be sure to include these. Purchasing agents like to know up front with whom you've done business. Obtain permission from satisfied customers to use their names for references for potential new customers. Describe your firm, including how long you've been in business.

## Management Expertise

The management expertise section should include resumés of the key members of your organization, outlining their training, education, and experience. How long has each member been with your firm? A uniform style for the resumés will enhance the professional image of your firm: There are countless books and Web sites that illustrate various common resumé formats and provide good guidance on preparing resumés.

## Research Capabilities

If your company does research, explain specifically what your capabilities include. This is important and could enhance your chances as a prospective supplier. If you don't have a division or staff dedicated to research, in this day and age it's incredibly easy to find people who do—consider establishing formal partnerships with people and firms who do research and development activities in your industry.

## Labor Relations

Describe the composition of your labor force. What is the average length of employment? If you have valued, long-term employees, it demonstrates the stability of your workforce, good working conditions, and most important, the probability of the continued availability of these people to your company.

Are your employees unionized? If your employees are unionized, a potential buyer might associate their higher skill levels with higher labor costs. To a potential buyer, the threat of a strike could prevent delivery of his orders. If there have not been any strikes at your company, be sure to include this point.

Is your business located in a state with right-to-work laws? Right-to-work laws prohibit "union shops," which require new employees to join the union. Wages might be lower with potentially lower labor costs. Are your employees paid minimum wage?

This might indicate easily replaceable employees and lower labor costs to a buyer.

Are both skilled and unskilled labor available for your business? A potential buyer wants to know how easily you can enlarge your staff to handle an order. A large labor supply indicates that your current employees will remain with you because of greater competition for available jobs. Manufacturers will particularly need to describe the availability of workers in their area. Also, list hourly rates of your current employees and the rates of any new additions to your workforce that might be necessary on the new contract you are seeking.

## Plant and Equipment

If appropriate for your firm, list the type of machinery that you use, including capacity, age, and number of each type. Photos of your plant or equipment are always helpful. Also, accurately list the size of your plant or office in square feet and your daily output when operating at your maximum level. This information might be requested by purchasing agents.

## Quality Assurance

If the customer has specifications you must meet—and nearly all will—explain how you will check and ensure that your product or service adheres to specifications. One way to demonstrate the integrity of your product or service is to offer a guarantee or warranty. If you do guarantee your service, describe the scope and how you will uphold it. Federal Express became famous for guaranteeing delivery of your package "when it absolutely, positively has to be there overnight." Now that is some guarantee and a magnificent obsession with commitment!

The wording of any guarantees or warranty should be checked with an attorney to ensure that you are not getting in over your head. Guarantees and warranties are strong marketing tools that can enhance your selling effort.

Big corporations want to know about your quality control program. If your firm has an established program to monitor the quality of production, or level of service provided, briefly describe it and its benefits to the recipient. Itemize any equipment used for testing and inspection and explain the tolerance, range, or capacity of the equipment employed.

## Financial Capability

Although you would probably prefer not to supply financial capability information, the corporate representative with whom you deal with will request a copy of your latest balance sheet, profit and loss statement, and line of credit information, if applicable. Others might also require your financial statements for the past three years. Even if your statements do not appear as healthy as you would like them to be, you cannot avoid this requirement. Thus, it pays to have them readily available.

## Price

Even without having a specific project to bid on, you will need to be prepared to give your prospect an overview of how you arrive at prices for your goods and services. Everyone is aware that prices depend on many variables; purchasing agents will want to get an overview of what the variables are for you. A successful prequalification package will identify and itemize factors affecting price, including setup fees, development and engineering charges, tooling and special equipment, testing fees, machine rates, personnel hourly rates, and so on.

A one-paragraph description of why the customer will be obtaining a good value for the price you are charging will strengthen your presentation. To meet the challenge of competition, offer your best price, along with your best quality and your best delivery date. While remaining competitive, you must strive to attain a minimum of deviation from the customer's requirements and your plans to meet them.

## Security

In many cases, you must be prepared to explain how you will guarantee that your prospective client's trade secrets, confidential information, or new product and service plans will be kept confidential. You may need to describe in detail the security measures in place for your plant, office, storage yard, or other facilities. How does your firm safeguard important documents, and who has responsibility for maintaining security? Your firm's ability to provide a high level of security to private-sector corporations will enhance your marketing position. This is particularly true if you deal with federal defense or aerospace contractors.

As I said at the beginning of this chapter, it's almost impossible to give you exact instructions about how to approach every large corporation—they each have their own unique methods and procedures for managing their purchases of goods and services. However, I hope I've helped you understand typical procedures and prepared you for the depth and intensity of the prequalification process. Now, in the next chapter I'll get specific to you, personally, and help you evaluate how well (or poorly) your own personal branding is working for you—if it's helping or hindering you from making the sales you want.

## Critical Points from This Chapter

- Ongoing, day-to-day collaboration with each client means that we're in the best possible position to serve our clients' current and future requirements. We're not merely providing a single service or product—we're integrated into the very fabric of each client organization.
- Most modern purchasing organizations look at their suppliers as strategic partners, not just providers of goods.

However, supplier performance—the tactical, day-to-day activity—is the responsibility of the purchasing department.

- Corporate purchasing personnel typically follow a comprehensive procedure for soliciting input, evaluating suppliers against the ideal and one another, and awarding contracts. In many cases, they prequalify a group of vendors who are then asked to bid against one another on a specific project.

- In most organizations, a committee of personnel review RFP responses and make collaborative decisions about contract awards.

- The most sophisticated large corporations and government agencies manage all aspects of buying from trusted suppliers electronically, with no paper exchanged at any point in the solicitation-purchase-payment timeline.

- The best first step you can take is to get in touch with the purchasing—or supply management—department of a corporation you're interested in and explain that you'd like to learn more about becoming a supplier.

- If the corporation has a small business supplier coordinator, consider this person your first and most important contact. If your prospect doesn't have a small business supplier coordinator, you have two other good options: (1) the top-most executive in charge of the business unit you're attempting to sell into and (2) the purchasing manager for the product or service you sell.

# What's Preventing You from Winning Big?

# It's Easy to Lose Perspective

Even if you handle the bidding and contracting process perfectly, you may not win business if you've lost your perspective. Many of us are prone to clinging too tightly to what got us "there" and made us successful, whereas others are so afraid of risk that they stick with what merely seems to work OK. There are a variety of common traps that business owners and salespeople fall into, and they all make it much harder for us to earn business from giant corporations and government agencies. Making yourself confront your bad habits and approaching sales to the giants with a strong, logical selling system will significantly improve your chances of winning big with the "big guys."

## Fire-Fighting Has Become a Way of Life

I know all too well the frustration of reaching the end of a day and realizing I've been "fighting fires" all day—answering client requests, handling personnel issues, and dealing with the normal day-to-day issues that face our business—without ever accomplishing the bigger picture things I had hoped to. Then, a week passes, and my list stays exactly as long as it was at the start of the week. In bad months, the entire month passes in fire-fighting mode. Sound familiar?

If you're wrapped up in the minute-by-minute of your business, it will be very easy for you to miss something important, whether it's new trends in your industry, a potential new client, or a competitor who's after one of your key customers. Unfortunately, I've seen talented salespeople miss—or even lose—great opportunities simply because they were mired in the minutiae of the day-to-day and were not taking the time to look at their business strategically *on a regular basis*.

I've learned that one of the most important things I can do is *make* the time and invest my effort to step outside of my day-to-day and think "bigger picture." A few suggestions:

- Have quarterly brainstorming meetings with your staff or project team. If you do this, you'll be amazed what you learn and where great ideas come from.
- Keep up with your reading—from popular business magazines such as *Inc.* and *Business Week* to industry-specific journals and white papers.
- Stay in touch with your clients. Ask them what they think you're doing well and what you could be doing better. Find out what new issues have come up in their businesses. (This can be a great way to earn more business, too!)
- Pay attention to what your competitors are up to. Look at their Web sites, promotional materials, and other publications regularly, check out their trade show booths, and talk to your peers about what they're observing about your competitors.
- Be creative about exploring unusual applications or unexpected clients for your products or services.

## Technological, Environmental, and Social Factors Affect Business

Today's suppliers find that if they're not paying attention, they'll get blindsided by technological, environmental, or social factors that can undermine their businesses. Think about these examples:

- Voice over IP communications systems—greater reliance on conference calls, lesser frequency of small on-site conferences.
- Collaborative supply chain systems—real-time communication enabled by Web-based technologies have transformed the way corporations source materials and services.

- The Green Movement—many of the giants, like Volvo, are asking that suppliers commit to exceeding specific environmental standards.

- Social networking—countless books and articles have been written about the phenomenon of social networking Web sites such as LinkedIn, Plaxo, Facebook, and others. Suffice it to say that most small businesses still haven't caught on to how to use these sites to their advantage!

These are just a few examples of the technological, environmental, and social factors that have come into play in the business world in recent years. I'm sure you can add many others to the list! The point is that as small business owners and salespeople, we should do everything we can to ensure that we have our fingers on the pulse of our industries and our clients' industries, and we should invest quality time into staying knowledgeable about the up-and-coming trends in business and technology.

## Costs Don't Always Change at a Predictable Rate

Energy costs are famously variable and often increasing. We saw the huge domino effect of increased gas prices in 2008, watching prices of everything from consumer goods to raw materials rise dramatically in a short period of time. The minimum wage has risen recently and is set to increase again. Health care costs rise every year and hit small businesses especially hard. One small business owner I spoke with recently told me that to provide decent, but not extravagant, health benefits to his 100 employees cost him more than $1 million during the fiscal year 2008. Existing government regulations cost the *average* business manager as much as 15 percent of his or her time and countless dollars, and in some more regulated industries far, far more. In the foreseeable future, the cost of water may rise dramatically.

When operating costs rise, savvy companies keep a close eye on their margins—remember, you can't make up lack of margin in extra volume. If your company experiences declining gross margin, it's a clear and inevitable signal that you are unable or unwilling to sell your products or services at a high enough price in comparison to the costs. Most organizations that file for bankruptcy due to operational reasons have had a clear history of declining gross margin significantly before they ever filed. They will often blame it on "cost increases," but the real culprit is a declining gross margin because their selling price was too low relative to their cost.

As one former business owner I know put it: "If I had increased price and cut capacity to half, we'd be in business today." His error, which he now sees, was that he did the exact opposite.

## What Worked before Will Not Necessarily Work Again

There's a great book by Marshall Goldsmith called *What Got You Here Won't Get You There*. In it, Goldsmith describes what he refers to as "The Success Delusion"—our belief that our past success is predictive of a successful future. We believe that our success is directly related to our actions and behaviors to this point, when in fact, that may be either partially or completely false. Successful people tend to have an unshakeable, almost superstitious belief that if they change anything about the way they act or think, their success will dry up.

In truth, past successes unfortunately have only limited meaning for the future, and the best defense, as always, is to stay flexible and roll with the punches. Resting too comfortably on past successes is probably the greatest area of potential trouble for suppliers, because what worked before may not necessarily have anything to do with current or future business requirements. In professional services, success can often be a function of the uneven distribution of competitors within a geographic area. For smaller manufacturers, success is often based on the fact that product sales are not sufficient for larger manufacturers to step in and overtake the particular market niche.

Merely relying on what has gotten you this far is a surefire recipe for failure. For small businesses especially, the importance of innovation, flexibility, and paying careful attention to the marketplace cannot be overestimated.

## The Myth of the Brand

I can't tell you how many times I've heard a salesperson complain, "We'll never get that account. We're up against XYZ company." It's true that many well-branded firms have the benefit of being perceived as "least-risk vendors" in the minds of their prospects and clients. But it's simply not true that small suppliers can't win business.

When most people think about a product or service being well branded, they think of the logo and marketing materials: Nike's swoosh, Apple's apple, the Maytag man, the Energizer bunny commercials, and so on. But "brand" really isn't just about a logo or a catchy advertisement. A brand is also about the promise you are making to your customers, the "feeling" they get when they think about using your product or service, the history of your company, and the benefits people believe they will get from using your product or service.

The best-branded products and services are firmly entrenched in our consciousness. If you've ever asked for a Kleenex, Xeroxed something, or ordered a Coke, you've been affected by strong brands. We have a saying here at The Brooks Group: "The stronger the brand, the weaker the sales force. The weaker the brand, the stronger the sales force." Imagine a Coke distributor and a new soft drink distributor trying to get a new corporate account: Who do you think will have to work harder to get the business?

Of course, there are many exceptions, because many exceptional salespeople work for well-known corporations and many awful salespeople work for companies with poorer branding. And many luxury products carry a luxury price tag that requires skillful selling to earn. However, here's the deal: If your firm isn't well-branded—or if it's had negative publicity for some reason—you're going to have to work longer, harder, and smarter than your better-branded competitors. But the great thing about being the owner or salesperson for a small firm is that you are *used* to working longer, harder, and smarter than your larger competitors. Everything you do has been challenging and hasn't had a precedent.

Small businesses just like yours can and do win business from the largest corporations and government entities. In 2007, $83.2 billion in federal prime contracts went to small businesses, and billions more went to small business subcontractors. Most large corporations have supplier development initiatives that seek to award contracts to small businesses.

The way to earn business from the "whales" is clear. It's not quick or even particularly easy, but it's logical and systematic. And it will help you win big.

## It's OK to Start Small in a Big Organization

Many years ago, we had the opportunity to provide sales training for a branch of a company that sells industrial pumps and compressors, which we did, and did well. That relatively small piece of business for us grew—and grew—as we were referred to other divisions of the firm and as the firm itself grew. Today we are the preferred sales and sales management training partner for the company, which is now a top 50 industrial distribution corporation.

In 2003, I was asked to provide a keynote address for a sales training conference put on by the largest long-term health care provider in the country. My speech there caught the attention of one of the company's vice presidents, who asked for our advice on structuring a comprehensive sales training program. That led to us not only building a customized sales training program and a train-the-trainer program for the organization, but also providing the firm with assessments for hiring and managing salespeople. Again, a relatively small contract—in this case, me speaking for an hour or so at a conference—led to a serious and mutually beneficial relationship with a huge corporation.

For many new salespeople, or those who are new to selling to the giants, large organizations can be overwhelming, simply because of their scale and complexity. And good luck getting in touch with the CEO of the firm—there are so many gatekeepers it's virtually impossible to make human contact! But the great news for all of us small businesses is that all giants are divided up into business units, each of which likely has its own decision-making authority. It's at that level that you are most likely to gain entry into the giant firms—at the division level. And it's also at that level that you're most likely to be able to serve the client well—few small firms have the capacity and infrastructure to perform nationally or globally without a significant investment of time and other resources.

If you can be taken seriously and provide exemplary service at the division level, your odds of being passed on to other divisions is extremely high. And in the process, you'll be building your capacity to service larger and larger accounts.

## Having a Strategy Is the Best Way to Ensure Success

It's a fact that large corporations are unwieldy, and they typically move slowly—decisions aren't made in a day (or even a month!). I recently read about a contract with a giant that had to be reviewed and signed by 21 people before a purchase order could be generated. Twenty-one people! So it makes sense that if you're interested in earning business from large organizations, you need a strong vision of what success means for your enterprise along with a high level of patience, and you have to be 100 percent systematic about the way you approach the marketing and sales processes.

First, and most important, you must have an excellent prospecting strategy for approaching and engaging these big accounts. However, *potential* business only translates into real dollars when you have a logical, intuitive sales strategy for working through the process of earning business. I'll talk a lot more about this throughout the rest of this book, but a good starting point is simply using a sales system. At The Brooks Group, we teach the IMPACT Selling System, but I'm here to tell you that using *any* system is better than using no system. In fact, salespeople who follow a linked, sequential sales process have a 93 percent chance of winning a sale, whereas those who do not use a system have only a 42 percent chance.

## Are You Talking to the Right People, and in the Right Way?

When you're selling to a small or midsized company, the person who has the authority to buy your product or service is likely to be a C-level or V-level manager. You've taught yourself how to get in front of these people, and odds are you know what messages work for you. But in a giant corporation or a government entity, there are entire staffs of people dedicated to purchasing—and the person who has the authority to generate a purchase order for your product or service may or may not have any decision-making power over the decision to outsource to you in the first place. One of our training programs—The Vital Salesperson—focuses on managing key and strategic accounts, and we've heard great feedback about the parts of this program aimed at helping salespeople navigate the corporate maze and knowing how to talk to the correct key executives.

In many cases, being selected to supply goods or services to a giant requires team selling on your part and team decision-making on theirs. One small business owner I know put a proposal in to a large corporation to do a relatively small amount of business—less than $50,000—on the request of a senior manager in one of the company's three divisions. The manager had the authority to select the vendor, but until the division's vice president, the purchasing department, and the legal department had signed off on the proposal, the vendor couldn't begin work. And the small business owner had to speak with three different company representatives, offer several professional references, and have her insurance agent speak with the legal department to get the final go-ahead.

In some cases, purchasing team members have authority to make decisions about suppliers, whereas in others, department personnel have spending authority up to a certain level, and in still others the purchasing department provides approved vendor lists to the entire company (and it practically takes an act of Congress to amend the list). That said, most A-list giants have sophisticated, efficient purchasing operations that are integrated into the supply chain, and these operations are staffed with intelligent, educated specialists. The goodwill of purchasing agents (or supply chain specialists, or purchasing managers, etc.) is essential to small business supplier success.

There are as many buying processes out there as there are companies. If you don't have an established relationship at another level in the firm, it's always a good idea to start as high up on the organizational chart as you can. If the executive with whom you make contact is willing to speak with you, simply ask him or her, "Whom should I talk to about becoming a supplier?" or "What is your buying process?" In some cases, you'll be able to develop a relationship with the executive, but in others you'll be passed down (or over) to someone in the purchasing area.

The late Tom Travisano, a gifted political pollster, and I worked hard over a long period of time to observe more than

12,000 sales interactions and then interview the decision maker afterward. The results were enlightening in many ways, and they require a book of their own to describe, but in short, we discovered that there are very specific ways in which unique buyer types want to be sold to. Purchasing managers, corporate executives, and facility managers each are a distinct category all their own, and we'll talk about them in much more detail in Chapter 8, discussing exactly which words, phrases, and messages are most effective with each.

## Being Afraid Limits Your Options

It's interesting. Salespeople and entrepreneurs are some of the bravest, most fearless professionals. They rely on their own personal strengths and trust their instincts every day—and yet when it comes to approaching the giants, most of them are afraid.

- Afraid of depending on a few big clients for the bulk of their company's revenue stream
- Afraid of being embarrassed by looking like a "small fish" in front of a big corporation's representatives
- Afraid of making the mental shift that's required to put the not-insignificant effort into prospecting and winning accounts with the giants
- Afraid of failure

You name it. And it's true, there are challenges associated with selling to the giants. But being afraid to even investigate the possibilities is one of the most self-limiting things you can do. In the next chapter, we'll talk a lot more about the mental side of selling to the giants and give you some help overcoming your fears.

## Critical Points from This Chapter

- Talented salespeople miss—or even lose—great opportunities simply because they get mired in the minutiae of the day-to-day and don't take the time to look at their business strategically *on a regular basis*.

- For small businesses especially, the importance of innovation, flexibility, and paying careful attention to the marketplace cannot be overestimated.

- It's true that many well-branded firms have the benefit of being perceived as "least-risk vendors" in the minds of their prospects and customers. But it's simply *not* true that small suppliers can't win business.

- If your firm isn't well branded—or if it's had negative publicity for some reason—you're going to have to work longer, harder, and smarter than your better-branded competitors.

- First, and most important, you must have an excellent prospecting strategy for approaching and engaging big accounts. But potential business only translates into real dollars when you have a logical, intuitive sales strategy for working through the process of earning business.

- In a giant corporation or government entity, the person who has the authority to generate a purchase order for your product or service may or may not have any decision-making power over the decision to outsource to you in the first place.

- Salespeople and entrepreneurs are some of the bravest, most fearless professionals. They rely on their own personal strengths and trust their instincts every day—and yet when it comes to approaching the giants, most of them are afraid.

# The Mental Side of Selling
# to the Giants

# Traits of the Giant Slayers

When I was a kid, I came in third in every race I ran. "Everyone" knew that there were two really fast boys—one of the two would always come in first, and the other would always come in second. I was always in third place, every time. Many years later, as I was coaching football, I remembered those races, and it dawned on me that I had been just as capable a runner as either of the other two boys. My problem was that I bought into the group's common knowledge that there were two fast runners, and I was not one of them. The group's expectations became my own expectations of myself; thus I was never able to outrun the other kids.

I never found out if I could beat them, because I never expected it of myself. This is hard to admit, even today, but I have seen many, many times over the years how powerful self-image and personal expectations are in shaping careers and personal lives.

A few years back, a bright, talented young lady named Sarah attended one of our IMPACT Selling seminars. She was new to the sales role, but no dummy and she had been doing a pretty good job of prospecting for business. She'd discovered that a business owner in her town was likely a strong prospect for the services she was selling. The guy was a big fish in her small town, and he was notoriously hard to get in touch with. She kept calling him and had left several voice mails.

At that point, she came through IMPACT training, and we talked during a break about getting involved in associations. I suggested that she find out in which membership organizations her prospect was active, and she'd already done her research: He was in the Lion's Club. So as soon as she got home after training, she joined the Lion's Club and volunteered for a committee.

Several months later, Sarah called me to give me the good news. She had just made a well-received sales presentation for the prospect she'd had no luck reaching months before. Here's what happened: While Sarah was helping on the committee she'd volunteered for, she had a legitimate occasion to call her prospect as a member of the Lion's Club to ask for his participation in a club project. During the call, she didn't mention her company. In fact, Sarah worked with her prospect as a volunteer for three months, and *never* mentioned her company.

One day, at a club meeting, Sarah's prospect overheard her introduce herself to a new member, at which point he asked her, "Why does your company name sound so familiar?" The rest, as they say, is history. Sarah's persistence, professionalism, and personal and professional integrity all came into play and earned her a tremendous opportunity. Her expectations were that she would win this account, sooner or later, and she was willing to position herself for success.

There are five common denominators that I see in the salespeople who are most successful at selling to the giants:

1. They have a total, unshakeable belief in themselves.
2. They have the ability to build trust and rapport with their prospects and customers.
3. They have a 100 percent commitment to and belief in the product or service they sell.
4. They follow a nonmanipulative, sequential selling process.
5. They are superior account managers.

## Belief in Yourself

No matter what your selling style, your prospects and clients will perceive how strongly you believe in yourself. Your confidence level and comfort as a salesperson show in every interaction you have with a prospect or customer. Every time you meet with someone, he or she subconsciously gathers information about you—in the first few seconds of your meeting (most research shows that this happens in the first 19–34 seconds!). Belief in yourself is so important that without it, the best trained, most professional salesperson may as well seek another profession.

You may have a superior product or service. You may have many wonderful selling skills. You may be managing or representing an exceptional organization. You may have hot prospects and a potentially lucrative sales territory. And you may have a fabulous network of contacts. But you will not be consistently successful in sales until you firmly and steadfastly believe in yourself.

## Trust and Rapport

It's a common misconception that salespeople need to be likeable. In truth, you will be much better served if your goal is to build trust and rapport with your prospects and customers. If you're aiming to be liked, you're much more likely to sell on price and lose your margins. The smartest salespeople seek to be trusted, and they sell value. There's a huge difference.

Think about it. Do you need to like your heart surgeon? Not really. But you do need to trust him or her to perform your bypass surgery with accuracy and precision. The world's worst heart surgeon might be the most likeable guy out there!

Odds are, if your prospects trust you, they will like you, too.

## Commitment to and Belief in Your Products and Services

If you drive a BMW, you can't sell a Lexus as effectively as the person who owns a Lexus, drives a Lexus every day, and loves his or her local Lexus service department. Knowledge, personal experience, and engagement with the products or services your organization sells all contribute to your credibility and likelihood of making a sale. In short: Salespeople who excel at selling to the giants are committed to and believe strongly in the products and services they sell. You must believe that what you offer your prospects is a sound investment and a good value for them. Remember, it doesn't have to be the best product or service on the market, but it has to be the *right* product or service, and at a price that is justifiable.

A word of caution here. Salespeople—particularly those with a technical product to sell—have a tendency to get feature-happy, touting the benefits of 800 features without ever finding out which of these features are most important to their prospect. I've seen many, many salespeople derailed because they were having a love affair with their product instead of really listening to what their prospects' requirements and desires were.

That said, enthusiasm and knowledge about your product or service is critical to success at sales. It just makes sense that your commitment to what you sell is transmitted to your prospects and clients. The enthusiasm you possess for what you sell is contagious; moreover, you can't feign it for any period of time.

There's a great, classic sales book by Frank Bettger called *How I Raised Myself from Failure to Success in Selling*, which was published in 1949. There are countless timeless stories in the book, but one of my favorites is early in Chapter 1. Bettger relates a story about increasing his income as a baseball player by 700 percent in 10 days, simply by deciding to establish himself as the most enthusiastic player out there. I'll quote him here:

> From the minute I appeared on the field, I acted like a man electrified. I acted as though I were alive with a million batteries. I threw the ball around the diamond so fast and so hard that it almost knocked our infielders' hands apart. Once, apparently trapped, I slid into third base with so much energy and force that the third baseman fumbled the ball and I was able to score an important run. Yes, it was all a show, an act I was putting on. . . .

Did it work? It worked like magic. Three things happened:

1. My enthusiasm almost entirely overcame my fear. In fact my nervousness began to work *for* me, and I played far better than I ever thought I was capable of playing.
2. My enthusiasm affected the other players on the team, and they too became enthusiastic.
3. Instead of dropping with the heat, I felt better during the game and after it was over than I had ever felt before. (Bettger, 5)

He goes on to describe how—after an injury stopped his baseball career—he was failing at sales until he realized that "the very fault which had threatened to wreck my career in baseball was now threatening to wreck my career as a salesman. The decision I made that night was the turning point of my life. That decision was to . . . put the same enthusiasm into selling as I had put into playing baseball."

I love this story because it illustrates how believing something and acting as if it's true can actually make it come true. Putting a smile on when you feel down really can help you feel happier, and feigning enthusiasm when you don't really feel it can generate genuine feelings of enthusiasm that inspire you—and others. Real enthusiasm can truly transform your life.

## A Nonmanipulative, Sequential Selling Process

Without a sales system, most sales professionals:

- fail to fully qualify leads, wasting prime time calling on un-qualified prospects.
- fail to investigate sales leads effectively prior to the first meeting.
- submit proposals and RFP responses without sufficient in-formation and preparation.

- waste the most crucial first three minutes of the sales meeting with small talk.
- launch into a needs-based "pitch" or proposal without uncovering deeper client motivations.
- fail to engage the client's deeper motivations, emotions, and imagination in the demonstration and application phases of the sales process.
- wait until price negotiations and closing the sale to think hard about how they should have set themselves up for success.

There's nothing like a game plan to transform scattered and uncoordinated sales efforts into an intuitive strategy. At The Brooks Group, we teach (and practice) the linked, sequential IMPACT Selling process, and I'll talk more about that in future chapters. Whether you use our system or another of the many reputable sales methodologies out there, you'll find that it helps you figure out exactly where you are in the sale and what move to make next.

Here's the principle: People always buy when they're ready to buy, not when you need to make a sale. If you're pursuing the largest corporations and government agencies, you know that there are countless details to keep track of during a lengthy sales process. Having a systematic approach like IMPACT Selling will help you get in front of qualified prospects and stay focused on the critical parts of the sale.

## Superior Account Management

Being systematic about account management is just as important as being systematic about the sales process, perhaps even more so. Large accounts require levels of coordination and attention to detail that smaller accounts may not require, especially if you're providing multiple products or services to the client. It's not just about winning the deal; it's also about keeping the business and building on it with follow-on projects and referrals to new prospects.

Every week, at least five Brooks Group employees have contact with one (or more) of about 10 people employed by one of our largest clients. Our salesperson acts as the account manager, but it would be unrealistic for him to be the single point of contact for every day-to-day issue. On any given day, our assessment interpreters will help a client hiring manager sort through job applicants, our curriculum design team might be working with client personnel to develop a new customized program, and our IT folks will be handling program registrations and online programs, while a facilitator is leading a telecoaching session with one of the client's sales teams.

In every one of these myriad touch points with our client, information is shared and gathered, successes and failures are experienced, and ideas and questions arise. If we didn't have regular status meetings involving everyone on our team who interfaces with our client's team, we would most certainly lose the account. If we didn't touch base regularly with the key point of contact on our client's end, we'd lose the account. And if we didn't have periodic "state of the project" meetings among our team and theirs, you guessed it: We'd lose the account.

We'll talk a lot more about account management in Chapter 11; for now, suffice it to say that ineffective account management will put your business in jeopardy, regardless of whether you choose to pursue the giants or stick with the small fry.

## What Values Have to Do with Success

Achieving anything in life requires that you have a set of values and principles that guide your course. The author William Faulkner once told a student, "I have found that the greatest help in meeting any problem with decency and self-respect and whatever courage is demanded is to know where you yourself stand. That is, to have in words what you believe and are acting from." Unfortunately, however, most people don't know what they believe and what they're acting on, and they are often (a) putting an incredible amount of energy into endeavors that don't really hold much significance for them or (b) not focusing their talents and abilities on the endeavors that *do* have significance for them.

At The Brooks Group, we've worked with literally hundreds of thousands of salespeople, sales managers, customer service personnel, and other business development personnel. And you know, I have been shocked by how few people have only the vaguest idea what their personal motivators really are or what truly rewards them, and how many people are investing precious energy and other resources into businesses or other pursuits that really don't reflect what they value. They often tell me they think they're "supposed to" pursue these things, yet they've never thought about *why* or where that notion came from. They've completely lost touch with their own values—and they're acting on expectations of others, others' ideas, and "group think."

## "Affectiveness"

We all are affected by—and affect—the people around us. We all do a little of both, being affected and affecting, but many times, we allow ourselves to be affected by others more than we strive to make an impact on them. If we allow this to happen, we're essentially allowing others to shape our futures and determine what's important to us. Let me be clear: Life's winners work hard to choose for themselves and influence others more than they are influenced by them.

Let me illustrate this another way. There's an ancient fable about a tiger who was orphaned after birth, but adopted by a herd of goats. Every day of his young life, the tiger played with the kids, drank goat milk, and slept with the goats. The little guy truly believed he was a goat, and he'd try as hard as he could to bleat like a goat, enjoy eating grass and paper, and play like a normal goat. But he just couldn't do it.

One day a huge Bengal tiger came bounding into the clearing where the cub was playing with the goats, and it let out a gigantic roar. All of the goats went scampering away, looking for cover, but for some reason, the little tiger felt drawn to this magnificent creature. Eventually, the big tiger led the cub down to the river and suggested that he look at his reflection in the water. The little tiger was amazed! Then, the big tiger sat back and let out a roar that shook the sky.

"There," he taunted the cub. "Why don't you roar like that?" So the little tiger strained as hard as he could. At first, he felt nothing, but then he began to feel a tiny rumble in his gut that grew stronger and stronger. At last, he opened his mouth wide and let out a gigantic roar of his own. From that day forward, he knew he could never live as a goat.

We all have a "tiger" inside—it's your deepest values and personal desires—and if you hope to be successful at selling to the giants (or at anything you do), you must connect with this tiger and never again settle for investing yourself in anything that doesn't get you closer to your goals or waste your energy on things that are inconsistent with your deepest values. That sounds so simple, but I am well aware that the simplest-sounding things are often the hardest.

## Ideal Versus Actual Values

We all have two kinds of values: ideal values and actual values. Ideal values are the lofty principles that we believe are driving our thoughts and actions. Actual values are those principles that really do drive us every day—and all too often, the actual values are quite different from the ideal values. I submit to you that the most successful salespeople are those who have defined and described their own ideal values to themselves and whose daily activities are guided by and support those fundamental values.

In other words, their actual values are extremely consistent with their ideal values.

This is a topic that fills many books, but let me give you a few questions that will start you on the path to restructuring your life around your ideal values:

- What is your personal definition of success? What would your life be like if you became extremely successful?
- What three principles most often guide your decisions and actions?
- What three qualities do you consider most essential for achieving success?
- What excites you more than anything else in the world?
- What frightens you most in the world?
- What is your primary consideration in making decisions about money, career, relationships, and time allocation?
- How much of your time are you investing in direct and active pursuit of your ideal of success?
- What will your life look like in 10 years if you continue in the direction you're currently going?

These are not simply idle questions. These are essential questions to answer if you hope to be a success at anything—whether it's selling to the giants or being a better parent. But merely answering them is not enough. Once you've given each question careful thought, it's time to get creative about finding ways to take action every day in ways that are consistent with your ideal values.

## Selling to the Giants Takes Creativity—Don't Block Yours

Another salesperson who attended an IMPACT Selling training program I led told me a funny story about gaining access to the decision maker at a firm with which he wanted badly to do business. Every time he tried to telephone the executive, he was rebuffed by the gatekeeper, the executive's administrative assistant. And she was not pleasant about it—after the third time he tried to get in touch with the executive—this time in person—the assistant literally told him that "as long as I am alive, you will not see this man," and she threw his card in the trash.

At this point, the salesperson knew he'd have to be creative. He was convinced that there was business there for him to win if only he could talk to the right person. So he decided to send a gorgeous bunch of flowers to the hard-edged administrative assistant, along with a note that said, "You're the most professional administrative assistant I've ever met. I want to acknowledge the good job you do." That's all it said, nothing more, and nothing less.

And guess what? It worked. The administrative assistant actually called the salesperson, and she said to him, "I see what you're trying to do, and it's total BS. But it worked. And I had to dig through the trash to get your card, and although I think the flowers were patronizing, I'll let you through anyway." A few days later, the salesperson had an amicable, productive introductory meeting with the executive!

Creativity is simply "producing through imaginative skills," and all of us have an imagination. Letting your past determine your future will lock you into patterns and hold you back from doing your best. It's all too easy to get bogged down, plodding along doing the same old–same old for months—even years—at a time. The good news is that every one of us has the creativity within us to break out of our molds and build the life that we want. The key is training our imaginations and using them to multiply our strengths and talents.

When you were a child, imagination was part of every day. You probably sat and daydreamed for hours, played with an imaginary friend, or fought imaginary demons in your backyard. But what has happened to all that creativity? Unfortunately, we grow out of it and begin focusing on the realities of day-to-day living.

Necessary, yes, but *not* taking some time to be creative and innovative may be preventing you from achieving those things you most want to achieve.

## Creativity Blockers

### Creativity Blocker #1: Too Much Routine

Look around your life. I guarantee you'll be able to find countless routines you go through for no good reason every day. You drive the same way to work every day. You have coffee at the same time every morning. You click aimlessly through e-mail after e-mail. Routine has a place in the world, don't get me wrong. But excessive and mindless adherence to routines breeds tedium and stifles creativity. Our minds crave stimulation, and when they don't get it, our thoughts settle into fixed patterns, and eventually we begin to believe that there's little we can do to change our lives.

### Creativity Blocker #2: Fatigue

I know so many successful, professional people who go home every night exhausted, eat a quick dinner, then collapse on the sofa only to fall asleep with the television on. What kind of life is that? What good does that do your relationships with friends and family? Where's your time for genuine rejuvenation and refreshment?

There are two types of fatigue: physical and emotional. Physical fatigue can be helped by sleeping more and better—it's amazing how much better I feel after a good night's sleep. Emotional fatigue brought on by excessive stress is more difficult to address, and it's also more destructive. It exhausts us and hinders all of our efforts to relax and rest. We get so caught up in the challenges and problems of life that we find ourselves struggling with the struggle itself.

## Creativity Blocker #3: Negative Thinking

An optimist sees an opportunity in every problem, but the pessimist sees a problem in every opportunity. Seeing yourself and your circumstances in a negative light can stifle any hope of applying your imagination to creatively solve the problems that plague you. Of course, life can be difficult. It's difficult for everyone, even the people who are born with silver spoons in their mouths, who seem to have everything going for them, and who have jobs you envy.

But life also is beautiful. It all depends on how you look at it. Negative thinking puts your creativity in cold storage and breeds a narrow-minded view of everything around you. Let me give you an example: I've had several employees who told me they hated coming late to work, yet were late virtually every day. When I asked them what they could do about being late, every one of them answered something like, "There's nothing I can do—it's just the way I am. I've always had a problem being late."

The real problem is that they've accepted the problem. By saying "That's just the way I am," they've closed off any possibility of finding a solution. They aren't able to ask themselves, "What can I change about my morning routine so I can get to work on time (or early)?" It's really no different to say to yourself, "I can't sell to XYZ Corporation. I've never had any luck with the big guys." Instead, you should be asking yourself questions such as, "What did I learn from my last attempt to sell to a giant?" and "What does ABC Corporation need that I can provide in a unique way?"

Negative people tend to reinforce one another, too. Many of the late-arrivers I confronted said, "I'm not the only one who comes in late" to defend themselves. We seek out people who have the same problems we do, and we develop an "us versus them" mentality. Unfortunately, the more you feed a negative attitude, the more it grows. One major concern can become a symbol of everything that you feel is wrong in your life and begin to consume you.

## Creativity Blocker #4: Fear

After the tragic *Challenger* space shuttle explosion, the news media interviewed several famous test pilots about the disaster, including General Chuck Yeager. I was captivated by his response to a reporter who asked, "When you discover that something has gone wrong, what do you do to keep from freezing up in panic?" Yeager answered, "You realize that you can't do anything to help your situation if you panic. It's foolish to worry about what you cannot control...so you get busy doing whatever you can to solve the problem.... That way you at least give yourself a fighting chance."

Fortunately, most of us don't face life-or-death situations on the job, but we do experience panic and stress brought on by our daily lives. For some salespeople, the thought of trying to approach the purchasing manager or chief operating officer of a major corporation practically makes them break out in hives. For others, the day-to-day stresses of managing accounts and pursuing prospects and handling rejection builds up over time. Whatever form it takes, fear is a deadly enemy to creativity—our resources get drained off by our efforts to overcome the immediate panic we feel.

## Creativity Blocker #5: Scapegoating

"If only I were smarter." "If only I had known whom to contact." "If only I hadn't missed the deadline." No matter what the problem, we tend to place blame for our failures on someone else or on some other factor than ourselves. Making excuses like these stifles our creativity because they shift the responsibility for finding solutions away from us.

## Popping the Cork on Creative Thinking

How do you become a truly creative thinker—and reap the rewards—in the face of so much negativity and pessimism? Here are some pointers:

1. Develop and maintain a creative mind-set.
2. Adapt—but don't conform.
3. Surround yourself with creative people.
4. Keep your mind uncluttered.
5. Maintain a steady flow of input/output.
6. Develop greater reasoning powers.
7. Try not to judge too quickly.
8. Focus on opportunities, not problems.
9. Recognize that you can choose how you react to setbacks.
10. Look at existing information in new ways.

# Enthusiasm: The Secret Ingredient

The word "enthusiasm" had been so overused that it's almost lost its original meaning. All the pep talks, motivational speeches, and empty slogans we're all exposed to have given us the feeling that enthusiasm equals "hoopla?"—pumped up hype that's shallow and short-lived. In truth, enthusiasm is a strong word with a rich heritage. It comes from an ancient Greek word, "ethos," which is loosely translated as "inspired by the gods," and it was coined to express admiration for athletes who performed what seemed to be superhuman feats. It literally meant a person who performed as if he or she had "a god inside them." (Think back to my Frank Bettger story.)

Enthusiasm grows up inside you or it doesn't exist: It comes from the inside outward, not vice versa. So how do you get inspired to achieve some overwhelming task—like selling to a giant corporation or government agency? Real, winning enthusiasm comes from a combination of two deep psychological factors: you're captivated by an ideal, and you have a deep conviction that you can do it.

## Being Captivated by an Ideal

Real enthusiasm springs from a strong belief that something is so worth doing that it demands the absolute best of your ability. What's more, the reverse is also true: Enthusiasm does not exist in the absence of a deep conviction that a task is one truly worthy of our best efforts. If you want to see your life really take off, give yourself completely to that deepest urge within you; lose yourself in the cause you consider to be worthy of your very best.

## Deep Conviction

The 1986 Super Bowl featured two excellent teams: The Chicago Bears and the New England Patriots. The teams were well-matched and either had the potential to win, but the Bears won a decisive victory. What was it that made the difference? It wasn't that the Patriots lacked the ability; sportswriters had been talking for years about the team's outstanding roster of talent.

Even back then, I believed you could spot the Super Bowl–winning difference in the two teams early in the season. All season long, the Patriot players and coaches had been making statements to the press about how they "hoped to at least make the playoffs." The week before the Super Bowl, some even confessed on television that they were happily surprised to be there. "I'm just glad for an opportunity to play in a Super Bowl," one of the players said.

But the Bears' opening game of the season had left little doubt in anyone's mind that they were a team that believed their time had come to win the big one. All season long, they exuded confidence that they not only would make the Super Bowl, but that they would bring home the trophy. They believed it was worth doing, and they had a deep conviction they could do it.

## Critical Points from This Chapter

- There are five common denominators in the salespeople who are most successful at selling to the giants:
  1. They have a total, unshakeable belief in themselves.
  2. They build trust and rapport with their prospects and customers.
  3. They have a 100-percent commitment to and belief in the product or service they sell.
  4. They follow a nonmanipulative, sequential selling process.
  5. They are superior account managers.
- Many, many salespeople derail because they are having a love affair with their product instead of really listening to what their prospects' requirements and desires are.
- Large accounts require levels of coordination and attention to detail that smaller accounts may not require, especially if you're providing multiple products or services to the client. It's not just about winning the deal, but about keeping the business and building on it with follow-on projects and referrals to new prospects.
- Life's winners work hard to choose for themselves and influence others more than they are influenced by them.
- Ideal values are the lofty principles that we believe are driving our thoughts and actions. Actual values are those

*(continued)*

*(continued)*

principles that really do drive us every day—and all too often, the actual values are different from the ideal values. The most successful salespeople are those who have defined and described their own ideal values to themselves, and whose daily activities are guided by and support these fundamental values. In other words, their actual values are extremely consistent with their ideal values.

• Enthusiasm grows up inside you or it doesn't exist: It comes from the inside outward, not vice versa. Real, winning enthusiasm comes from a combination of two deep psychological factors: you're captivated by an ideal, and you have a deep conviction that you can do it.

# Positioning Yourself to Sell
# to the Giants

Let's say you've successfully completed the vendor/supplier prequalification process with a giant corporate prospect, either through the purchasing department or by building credibility with a company executive or two. You're periodically receiving requests for proposals or inquiry calls from purchasing personnel—is that a guarantee you'll win contracts? Of course not. Jumping over the initial hurdle doesn't eliminate your competition—in fact, it virtually guarantees you're up against competitors who have just as strong an offering as you do! At this point, you need to be considering each unique opportunity with the corporation as a new sales process, with a beginning, middle, and end.

Once you know there's a potential contract for you—whether you've been prequalified or not—you should approach the opportunity exactly as you would any other sales opportunity: systematically. I've said it before, and I'll say it again: If you want to play big, you've got to show that you can play with the big guys. Everything about you should signal to your prospects that you are 100 percent capable of fulfilling the promises that you make to them. I don't mean that you should be arrogant or presumptuous; but you should be professional, prepared, and proactive in all of your dealings with a prospective client. To do that consistently and effectively, you have to be organized and diligent, and following a sales system is the easiest way to do that.

We teach hundreds of IMPACT Selling courses every year to salespeople in all walks of life. Time and time again, people tell me that there are two things that stand out to them about the sales system we teach:

1. We talk a lot about what happens before you ever make contact with a prospect—the positioning and precall planning that will ensure you're ahead of the game before you even make contact with your prospect.
2. We don't just talk about prospects' *needs*. Instead, we work to find out the prospects' *wants*.

We'll talk a lot more about the second one in the next chapter. For now, suffice it to say that people sometimes buy what they need, but they *always* buy what they want. In this chapter, I want to concentrate on positioning yourself both before and during the formal sales interactions you have with representatives of giant corporations—whether they're purchasing managers, administrative support staff, or top executives.

## Why Is *Your* Personal Positioning So Important?

Most people assume that it's their company's positioning in the marketplace that's most critical, and it's true . . . if you have a well-known product or your company is virtually a household name, you have an initial advantage simply because of name recognition. But you'd be surprised how short-lived that advantage is. The truth is that strong *personal* positioning can absolutely, positively win large accounts for your firm, even if you own or sell for a small, little-known company. The inverse is true, too: Poor personal positioning can lose potential opportunities even for the best-known, strongest companies.

Your personal positioning can supersede your product's, service's, or even your organization's positioning. To your prospects and customers, YOU are your product, service, and organization. Every interaction that they have with you—whether it's in person, via mail, or virtual—tells them something about your company and its capacities. If they perceive you to be honest, organized, efficient, responsive, and professional, odds are that they'll also believe those things to be true of your company. Their subconscious logic tells them that a person with all of the good traits you exhibit would never work for a company that was disorganized, inefficient, slow to react, and unprofessional.

## It's Easy to Misposition Yourself—or Not Position Yourself at All

It's interesting that most old-school salespeople will tell you that closing is the most essential part of the sale—and there are countless articles, books, and seminars out there teaching salespeople myriad ways to close the deal. But our research has shown over and over again that the opposite is the case. How you *open* the sales process is the most critical step toward winning a new contract. Opening the sale is effectively all about personal positioning. And personal positioning is all about creating such a strong, positive presence, awareness, and recognition in your buyers' minds that they always think of you first and most receptively when they are ready to make a purchasing decision about your product or service.

Salespeople are notorious for being poorly positioned. Do any of these descriptions sound like any salespeople who have called on you?

- Pushy
- Desperate to make a sale
- Fast-talking, not listening
- Quick to "negotiate" price
- Pushing whatever product or service is newest (or gives them the greatest commission), instead of what you really need
- Feature-happy

It amazes me that in training sessions, I can ask participants to list negative traits of salespeople, and they can do it in an instant; but when I ask them to come up with positive traits, it takes them a lot longer to answer. And these are people who have chosen sales as a career!

Almost as bad as being poorly positioned is *not* being positioned. If you're not positioned at all in your prospects' minds, they simply don't think of you when they have a project or a requirement with which you could assist them. Too often, salespeople just don't think about investing their time and effort into personal positioning. It simply doesn't occur to them.

Think about the best salespeople you know. What do they do that impresses and inspires you? Here are a few things that spring to my mind:

- Attentive and responsive to requests for information or service
- Good listener
- Scrupulously honest, both personally and professionally
- Goes above and beyond; may assist with things outside the scope of the current contract
- Appreciative of his or her clients
- Excellent attitude, seeming friendly, and appropriately relaxed

A salesperson who had these traits would likely be well positioned in his or her prospects' and clients' minds. The salespeople on my team here at The Brooks Group usually do a fantastic job of positioning themselves with their prospects and customers—and we're stronger for it. Our clients often think of us first (and only!) when they have new projects arise, and it's because everyone from the sales team to the support staff here go out of their way to position themselves and our company well.

## A Quick Positioning Audit

If you're already engaged with a giant corporation or government agency, rate the following statements on a scale of 1 to 5 (with 1 being the least and 5 being the most). If you're just in the initial stages of dialogue with a giant, consider these statements to be goals for your new account.

| | |
|---|---|
| I have had discussions at the senior management level about the future direction of my prospect's organization. | |
| My key contacts are in positions that have access to future plans and directions. | |
| My key contacts and I mutually share valuable information whenever we meet. | |
| My key contacts actually suggest that we have meetings with other key decision makers. | |
| My key contacts believe our product or service should receive preferred selection or vendor status. | |
| My key contacts clearly know how our product or service can provide superior solutions and actively work to further their agenda. | |
| My key contacts have helped me understand the protocol, procedures, and policies related to how his or her organization buys products or services. | |
| My key contacts allow me the latitude to openly suggest meeting with others whose position can be improved through the use of our products or services. | |
| My contacts know the strengths, weaknesses and correct applications of our product or services that exceed—more than simply meet—immediate needs. | |
| Total | |

**Now, look at how your score translates into the perceptions your contacts have of you:**

- 9–24 points: You're seen as an enemy in their midst. You are not demonstrating that you have significant value to add, and they are unlikely to pursue doing business with you.

- 25–34 points: You're perceived as a mild to severe adversary. Things could go either way for you, depending on how well you handle yourself and the sales process from this point forward.

- 35–45 points: You have built strong internal advocacy. You are well positioned and have a high likelihood of winning business from this prospect. It's not in the bag, but it's yours to lose.

## Positioning Tips

Every salesperson or executive who needs to develop business has his or her own strengths and talents. This is especially true when you're selling to the giants because in most cases, you have to position yourself with multiple people within the organization so that you're top of mind for all of them. There are hundreds of ways you can work with your own abilities to position yourself in ways that make you a recognized expert and resource for your prospects and clients. I encourage you to come up with your own ideas for improving your positioning, but here is a list of my top 10:

1. Develop a list of 30 to 40 prospects and customers to whom you will send a monthly article, update, tip sheet, small gift, or other relevant professional item.

2. Join and be active in associations in your own industry and those of your prospects and clients.

3. Offer free, how-to-do-it, noncommercial seminars or workshops for associations and organizations to which your prospects belong.

4. Become a columnist for trade magazines and journals that your prospects and customers read.

5. Write and widely distribute a "how-to" manual that helps your customers do what they do better.

6. Collaborate in strategic partnerships with noncompeting products or services to be seen as a total solution that will serve your mutual prospects' problems.

7. Develop and distribute your own monthly or quarterly electronic newsletter to targeted prospects.

8. Build and promote your own Web site with free information and helpful tips for your customers and prospects. Be sure to keep it up-to-date and relevant.

9. Serve on boards and committees that have high visibility with your targeted prospects.

10. Sponsor activities that are attended by people in your target market.

Before you get overwhelmed: Don't try to do all of these at once! Pick one or two that you think will work best for you, and pursue them with all your might. If you don't personally have the expertise to do what you want to do, get help from others and make it happen.

## Trade Shows and Other Association Activities: Acres of Diamonds

One of the absolute best possible ways to grow your business is participating in industry associations and activities such as trade shows. If you're doing your research and staying on top of what's going on in your own industry and those of your clients, you'll know which trade and professional groups are respected the most. Join these groups, but don't stop there. Involve yourself on a committee that will allow you to interact with potential clients. Volunteer to write a quarterly column for an association's newsletter—you'd be surprised how easy this is to do, and how hungry publishers are for content. Present a how-to session or participate on an expert panel at an association convention or meeting.

## A Warning: Slow Down

Let me be clear about something here. Your participation in these groups does *not* give you carte blanche to go in with sales guns blasting. If you begin haranguing other members at your first meeting about sales leads, or you're constantly sending out e-mail blasts to the association mailing list, you're not adding any value, and you're positioning yourself poorly. If you participate actively and intelligently, and you position yourself and your firm as experts with significant knowledge to impart, people will begin approaching YOU—no hard sales "pitch" needed.

## Some Advice about Attending Conferences and Trade Shows

Attending conferences and trade shows has many potential benefits that justify the cost of attending and the time away from your office. These events:

- can enable you to contact a large number of prospective buyers in a short time.
- give you the opportunity to see potential competitors and the products/services they are offering.
- may give you ideas for a new product, service, or method of distribution.
- enable you to gain experience in dealing with prospective clients, revealing areas of a presentation that need clarification, products or services that are desired from a prospective buyer, modifications that would enhance a product's demand, and so on.

To come away from the show with a list of blue chip prospects for follow-up—people who might not actually buy or sign up for anything on the spot, but who are worth your time in terms of follow-up contacts—requires planning, organization, and follow-up. Start well before the event by reviewing a list of event attendees, selecting your potential prospects. Send these prospects, ahead of time, some information about your company and an invitation to meet with you at the event.

Follow up with phone calls; attempt to arrange specific times to meet with some of the individuals you have targeted during the week of the show. The group you have targeted for their high potential will, during the show, slowly narrow down to a smaller group of actual prospects—people you'll keep in touch with after the trade show.

Plan your time at the show carefully, visiting the organizations you would like as customers. Maximize your time by visiting the press or information area and obtaining a list of exhibitors and their locations. Talk with the exhibitors who could be likely customers for you but don't come on too strong because they're the ones exhibiting—not you. Simply leave your business card.

If there is time and the corporate reps are not too busy obtain the names, addresses, and phone numbers for the small business vendor coordinator or appropriate purchasing agent. Try to procure copies of supplier lists for use in identifying potential customers for your firm. You may not be able to get all of this information as a visitor. However, the contact you've made is still valuable.

Once you are back in your office, be sure to follow up on whatever contacts or information you've developed. The contacts you've met also met 200 other people at the show, so your follow-up must be swift, informative, and professional.

## Staying in Touch

We have an unfortunate tendency to feel that there's nothing we can do for a prospective giant corporation until the time an actual, biddable opportunity arises for us to pursue. That couldn't be farther from the truth. As I said in the preceding section, personal positioning is an ongoing effort and one that usually pays off richly. But the people who are best at selling to the giants do something else critical: They help their clients find ways to use their products or services. This goes hand in hand with the notion of corporations looking to suppliers as strategic resources.

Corporate purchasing personnel *want* you to add value and make reasonable recommendations. They *want* you to be innovative and help them operate intelligently and efficiently. Oftentimes, you can show that by giving you the opportunity to provide a product or a service, the purchasing organization can save themselves time, money, hardship, opportunity costs, inventory expenses, and so on. But they won't know that—and you won't know you have a business opportunity—if you aren't regularly interacting with your prospects' purchasing executives.

If you have the benefit of having a small business program liaison at your prospect's headquarters, they can be the best resource you've got. Most of the time, they're receptive to small business owners and salespeople and will help you make the proper contacts within their organizations. If you're not so lucky, you still need to do your best to make inroads into the corporation, speaking regularly with key contacts who might be potential users of your products or services.

## Getting (and Keeping) Your Foot in the Door

Whether you're currently doing business with a giant or seeking your first contract, you must apply everything you've learned about positioning yourself (and your company) as the solution provider of choice. Even if you've built a basic relationship with your prospect by getting certified or prequalified as a service provider or product vendor, you'll have to make the effort to meet with the organization's personnel to discuss ideas and learn about upcoming projects that may be relevant to you. You can't assume, however, that everyone in the corporation knows that you've gotten prequalified or that your firm has something of value to offer. With each contact you make in the organization, you should be prepared to start fresh—just as you will be doing if you're seeking business from a corporation or government agency that doesn't have a prequalification process.

## People of Influence

In virtually every organization—from small to enormous—there are multiple decision-making levels, from the CEO and similar executive functions on down to the line manager or supervisor level. If the corporation you're hoping to sell into has a formal purchasing process, by all means follow it. But don't let that limit your contact in the firm to the purchasing manager or buyer with whom you've been assigned to work. The most successful salespeople find ways to work in accounts high enough to create legitimate authority and reinforce strategic partnership status and, simultaneously, deeply enough to create internal pull for what they sell. If they only have a relationship at a lower management level, they use their products and services to make their primary contact look good while advancing themselves in the organization.

This may or may not surprise you, but each level of management has a very different fundamental rationale for buying. This is really the subject of an entire other book, but let me give you a quick overview of what we've found:

- CEOs, presidents, and many senior VPs buy primarily on strategy and big picture.
- Directors, senior managers, and most VPs buy primarily on implementation and getting results.
- Managers, supervisors, and other lower-level decision makers buy primarily on maintaining functionality of systems and people they manage and avoiding unnecessary work.

**Level I.** Buys on Strategy
**Level II.** Buys on Implementation
**Level III.** Buys on Price

**FIGURE 7.1** The Decision Maker Pyramid

If you're seeking business with a progressive corporation or government agency, the senior VP of supply management may be your best possible contact point. He or she will likely have the authority to make strategic decisions about sourcing products and services and be willing to consider new or innovative uses for what you sell. Your day-to-day contact with the giant may be at a lower level, but I strongly encourage you to make the effort to strategize with the most senior-level person you can on a regular basis. Regardless of whom you're calling on, you should keep their decision-making level in mind and craft your messages in terms that will appeal to their primary buying motives. (We'll talk a lot more about this in the next chapter.)

There are two very specific statements that I find essential to making contact with key personnel and ensuring their receptivity to meeting with you. The first is the direct value statement, and the second is the statement of intention. I'll describe each in detail and explain how to use them.

## The Direct Value Statement (DVS)

A direct value statement (DVS) briefly, clearly, and declaratively communicates the fundamental reasons why your organization exists and why you are selling its products or services. If you have a DVS prepared, you can leave a confident, effective voice mail or e-mail, or get to the point of a face-to-face visit rapidly and efficiently. The DVS is both a positioning tool, explaining in a nutshell about your firm and an advertising tool, along the lines of a 30-second commercial.

### The basic form a DVS takes is:

- "We assist clients [or customers] in the _____ industry [or business] to _____. We do this by _____."

### Here are a few examples:

- "We assist clients in the finance industry to reduce turnover. We do this by assessing potential employees for 'fit' to their companies and then training them to win business from profitable accounts."
- "We assist clients in the construction equipment manufacturing industry to improve productivity. We do this by redesigning and documenting processes for greater efficiency and safety."
- "We assist clients in the wireless phone business to reduce inventory costs. We do this by providing just-in-time inventory plans with total transparency via Web-based tools."

People will choose to do business with you if they believe you can reduce or remove a problem, solve an issue, improve a situation, or strengthen their position. Can you describe why your company exists and what you do in two sentences? If not, work on it. Depending on what you sell, you may be able to come up with a "one size fits all" DVS; if you sell a variety of products and services in multiple industries, you should craft unique DVSs for each key segment of your market. Here are four questions that will help you develop your own DVS:

1. Do you work with individuals, organizations, associations, government agencies, or other groups?

2. Do you specialize in certain markets? Industries? Types of businesses?

3. What do you help your customers do? Gain market share? Reduce costs? Improve productivity?

4. How do you help your customers? By improving processes? Improving yield? Providing upgraded equipment? Training?

A DVS is one of the most important tools in your sales toolbox. It can make the difference between getting an appointment with a key executive or getting shut out. And it is an essential positioning tool that sets positive expectations in your prospects' and clients' minds, whether you've never met them before or you've met them many times.

## The Statement of Intention

What are you trying to accomplish when you call or visit a prospect or customer? In which step of the sales process are you? Before you make a telephone call or sales call to a company from which you're hoping to earn business, think carefully about why you're putting yourself in front of your prospect and what your goals are for the call. Are you hoping to be considered a prime supplier for an organization or agency? Are you seeking clarification about an upcoming RFP? Are you hoping to suggest a new product or service to an existing client?

In our study of thousands of sales interactions, we found that 95 percent of decision makers found small talk to be negative or neutral. Small talk virtually never helps you achieve your goals. Instead, I encourage you to use a statement of intention to establish trust and rapport with the person you are calling on by setting expectations and removing pressure. A statement of intention helps you get what you want by making it clear to your prospects and customers who you are, why you're there, and what's in it for them to talk with you.

**Here are a few examples:**

- **For a New Prospect or a New Contact:**
  "What I'd like to accomplish today [or in our meeting] is to meet you, ask you a few questions, and see if I may be of service. We work hard to ensure that all of our clients/customers get exactly what they want, and that's how I'd like to work with you. Does that sound OK?"

- **For an Existing Customer:**
  "What I'd like to accomplish today [or in our meeting], if it's OK with you, is to spend a little time together, ask you a few questions, and see if there's a way that I can be of further assistance to you. Does that sound OK?"

If you are really brave, there's something else here that will tell your prospect or customer how serious you are about making sure you add value for them, and that you truly are focused on their needs and wants. What is it? Add the following phrase to the end of your statement of intention:

- "If together, we find that I can't help you, I can certainly recommend someone else who can."

In some training groups, when we present this phrase, there is either stunned, uncomfortable silence, or outright laughter.

But let me tell you, if you are committed to winning business from the big guys, this simple phrase can be your ticket. It immediately signals to your prospect or client that you want what's best for them, not just yourself. And it positions you as someone who is a strategic resource with a variety of valuable contacts, not just a "one-hit wonder."

The catch is that you have to be willing to do it—to refer your prospect to someone who can help them if you can't or can't do it well. It's really hard for salespeople to consider doing that, but it's another tool that emphasizes your position as a resource and an expert in your field. If you put your prospect or customer in touch with a resource they need, it makes *you* look good! (And truthfully, as afraid as salespeople are to say they can't help a prospect or customer, it really doesn't happen all that often, especially if you've qualified your prospects effectively.)

Here's a perfect example from our sales training world. Many times, when we've advised a client that a potential hire was not going to be a fit for their environment (based on our battery of assessments), the client has asked if we knew any reputable recruiters. For years, we had to admit that we really couldn't recommend a solid placement firm (and frankly, we didn't want to, as many of them offer assessments of their own). However, one of our salespeople recently built a relationship with a proven placement agency and created a solid cross-referral agreement. Now, when asked if we can recommend a recruiter to one of our assessment clients, we say "absolutely!" And on the other side of the coin, we're finding that our recruiter advocate is sending assessment business to us!

## When You Can Put Them Together

Imagine you're calling the purchasing manager at a giant corporation you're hoping to do business with. You've done your research to ensure that you're calling on a truly qualified prospect.

Here's how you'd use the DVS and the Statement of Intention in your initial phone call:

- "Hi, Frank. My name is Susan, with XYZ Company. We help clients in the apparel industry get sustainably produced fabrics at the best prices. We do this by handling the legwork and managing the sourcing process for them."
- [Prospect will likely greet you in return.]
- "I'd like to have the opportunity to talk with you, ask you a few questions, and see if I may be of service to you. We work hard to ensure that all of our customers get exactly what they want, and that's exactly how we'd like to potentially work with you. However, if together, we find that I can't help you, I can certainly recommend someone else who can."

In a few short sentences, you've articulated to your prospect why he should consider talking with you further or meeting with you in person. You've positioned yourself and your firm well, and you've put your prospect at ease that you're not a "typical" fast-talking, pushy salesperson. What could be better?

## Precall Planning: Being Prepared

Congratulations, you've earned the opportunity to meet with a key decision maker. If you're a small fish calling on a big whale, you definitely need to do your homework. Nothing should take you by surprise when you're meeting key decision makers, and you should maintain the strong personal positioning you've worked hard to develop up to this point. This is not the time for showing off, being pushy, or making blind assurances you can't really support. Rather, this is the time for smooth, calm professionalism and 100 percent attention and focus on your prospect.

In Chapter 3, I gave you some advice about profiling your prospects, but here are a few more suggestions for effective pre-call planning when you have a set appointment:

- **Do exhaustive research about the company you're calling on.** Take advantage of the Internet and the reference librarian at your local library. Study your prospect's annual reports, newsletters, press releases, and other materials. Do a search for recent articles about the company, and talk to peers who've won business from it. Determine who key personnel are and how the organization is structured.

- **Prepare your statement of intention for the meeting.** What is your goal for the meeting, and why is it in the prospect's interest?

- **Develop a list of questions to ask the person with whom you'll be meeting.** Even if you don't use them all, you'll be glad you have them as a reference.

- **Ensure you have all of your key sales tools and aids packed and ready to go.** It may be helpful for you to create a checklist of everything you typically use.

- **Confirm your appointment the day before.** Be sure you know exactly where you're to meet, and who will be there—just the decision maker or other people as well?

## Critical Points from This Chapter

- If you want to play big, you've got to show that you can play with the big guys. Everything about you should signal to your prospects that you are 100-percent capable of fulfilling the promises you make to them.

- Strong *personal* positioning can absolutely, positively win large accounts for your firm, even if you own or sell for a small, little-known company. The inverse is true, too: Poor personal positioning can lose potential opportunities even for the best-known, strongest companies.

- Personal positioning is all about creating such a strong, positive presence, awareness, and recognition in your buyers' minds that they always think of you first and most receptively when they are ready to make a purchasing decision about your product or service.

- Know which trade and professional groups are respected the most in your clients' industries. Join these groups, but don't stop there. Involve yourself on a committee that will allow you to interact with potential clients. Volunteer to write a quarterly column for the association's newsletter. Warning: Do *not* go in with sales guns blasting. Be an active, intelligent participant.

- The people who are best at selling to the giants do something critical: They help their clients find ways to use their products or services.

- Buying motives at each management level are different:

  - CEOs, presidents, and many senior VPs buy on strategy and big picture.

  - Directors, senior managers, and most VPs buy on implementation and getting results.

  - Managers, supervisors, and other lower-level decision makers buy on maintaining functionality of systems and people they manage and avoiding unnecessary work.

- The form of a direct value statement (DVS): "We assist clients [or customers] in the _____ industry [or business] to _____. We do this by _____."

(continued)

(*continued*)

- A statement of intention sounds like this: "What I'd like to accomplish today is to meet you, ask you a few questions, and see if I may be of service. We work hard to ensure that all of our clients/customers get exactly what they want, and that's how I'd like to work with you. Does that sound OK?"

- Don't forget this statement: "And if together, we find that I can't help you, I can certainly recommend someone else who can." It's a big thing to promise, but the rewards for doing so can be tremendous.

# Learning the Buyer's Language

In the last few chapters, we've looked at how giant corporations and government agencies buy and how to position yourself for success at selling to them. Now, to target and reach specific prospects, you'll need to ensure that you understand the language your key contacts speak and have strong selling techniques that address the unique motivations of the people who perform each buying role. What you'll learn in this chapter is backed up by our research with thousands of decision makers in a wide array of industries. It's been tested and proved to work.

Years ago, a vice president of engineering told me, "Every salesperson talks about what I need. I'd much rather talk about what I *want*." In the years since that comment, I've come to see that success in building an effective message is completely, totally dependent on understanding that prospects—whether purchasing agents, CEOs, or "the person on the street"—don't always buy what they need, but they always, *always* buy what they want.

Why is this so important for us as salespeople and small business owners to understand? Because at the core, you're not selling to a giant corporation. You're selling to an individual or group of individuals who represent the corporation but are motivated by their own unique psychological requirements and professional desires. Yes, you ought to have an account plan that looks strategically at the giant's operation, structure, and procedures, but what's most important any time you interact with a decision maker is that you relate comfortably and professionally with him or her, addressing his or her most fundamental needs *and* wants.

What exactly those needs and wants are depends on many factors, but they're strongly correlated with (a) the role an individual plays within an organization and (b) the position he or she has in the decision-making process to use (or not use) your company's product or service. One of the most important tools you should be using is an Influence Map that helps you keep track of key personnel and target individuals' unique requirements and desires. Once you've determined what motivates each key player, you'll be able to convey your message in the way that they want to hear it—opening the door for you whether you're speaking with a purchasing manager or a corporate executive.

## What Decision Makers Need (and Want)

Unfortunately, the distinction between needs and wants is one that most salespeople and business owners never understand, let alone master. Chances are, you've read a book or two on selling. Maybe you bought some videos or audios on the topic, and you've probably sat through a couple of sales training programs. Almost all the books, seminars, training programs, and audios in the world talk about the same thing. They teach you how to fulfill the age-old promise that salespeople make to decision makers:

"I want to meet your needs."

Of course, it's pretty obvious that you can't build a career on giving decision makers what they *don't* need. You can't sell landscaping services to someone who lives in a high-rise, or software to someone who doesn't know how to use a computer, or an MRI machine to a machine shop. The decision maker's needs are, obviously, a vital part of the sales process and of the buying decision. But they are not the only vital element of how decisions are made. Decision makers also have (often unspoken) *wants* that come into play when they are making choices about what to purchase. Your sales success is directly related to how well you can uncover not just what your prospects *need*, but also what they *want*.

Let's look at needs and wants side by side:

| Needs | Wants |
|---|---|
| Application-related | Personal |
| At the surface | Below the surface |
| Rational | Emotional |
| Fact-oriented | Perception-oriented |
| Product- or service-specific | Not product- or service-specific |

**Needs are:**

- Application-related: Let's say you're selling a piece of diagnostic imaging equipment, maybe an MRI system. You could satisfy a hospital administrator's need to replace an outdated piece of equipment with your new MRI system.

- At the surface: Decision makers are well aware of their needs and will talk about them openly, and they know that their needs are directly related to their buying decisions.

- Rational: It makes sense to buy an MRI if you need one. It's rational for a decision maker to satisfy his or her needs.

- Fact-oriented: Needs are not based on theory or conjecture, and given enough information, any intelligent person can figure them out.

- Product- or service-specific: You can't use a piece of prime real estate to satisfy a decision maker's need to run industrial fluids and gases through narrow piping in a factory. You need a good tube connector for that. Real estate can satisfy some other need, but not this one.

You have to know what the decision maker's needs are. You will have to address them and ultimately satisfy them. Just don't be obsessed with them. In other words, don't buy the story that decision maker needs are the total package, the complete sum and substance of the buying decision. If you only address needs—and ignore the wants—you'll continue to experience all of the frustrations that drive salespeople crazy.

So what are *wants*? Let's talk about this other side of the coin—the one thing sales theorists, experts, trainers, gurus, and writers never deal with.

## Wants Are Personal

In contrast to needs, which are application-related, decision-maker wants are personal in nature. Having better cash flow (need) is good for almost everybody who's associated with an entrepreneur's business. However, the entrepreneur *wants* personal independence so she can keep collecting a respectable paycheck and have no boss attached to it. If you can show the entrepreneur how your solution accomplishes both her wants and her needs, everybody wins.

## Wants Are Below the Surface

We said earlier that decision makers are very aware of the direct relationship between their needs and the buying decisions they make. You can't say the same for wants. In fact, some research I did showed that decision makers choose to reveal their wants to the salesperson *less than 2 percent of the time*. Decision makers simply don't talk about their wants with salespeople the way they talk about their needs. Why? Because most decision makers have no real idea how much their wants affect their buying decisions, so they ignore them because they perceive them as irrelevant to the purchase. (They aren't.)

## Wants Are Emotional

Wants are big emotional issues for decision makers, and in most cases, they have little relationship to rational priorities or concerns. We asked more than 1,400 business owners this question: "If you could have a job with a large company that pays you double what you make now, gives you a generous expense account, a complete benefits package, and a strong retirement plan, would you give up being an entrepreneur?" We purposely selected entrepreneurs whose businesses weren't in good shape, but despite that, 94 percent gave us a flat out "no" answer. The emotional gratification of being independent was far more powerful than any amount of money or security. But most of them would never have thought that their emotions come into play in their decision-making processes!

## Wants Are Perception-Oriented

Instead of being fact-oriented, like needs, wants are tied into the decision maker's perceptions. We'll discuss exactly how they fit together later.

## Wants Are Not Product- or Service-Specific

The decision maker's wants cut across all product and service lines. Think of them as the "emotional baggage" decision makers carry with them into every sales interaction and buying decision.

# Five Types of Wants

There are five specific wants every prospect has, regardless of the product or service they may need. Your job is to use the right phrases to describe and position each want before you actually present your product or service. What the right phrases are will depend heavily on the position of the individual you're speaking with and what his or her decision-making role is. Here are the five wants:

- **Primary Want:** The type of relationship the prospect wants to have with a salesperson, supplier, or vendor. ("I want buying your product to make me look good to my peers.")
- **Product or Service Want:** The way the prospect wants to perceive the product or service he or she seeks. ("I want your product to be easy to use—not too technical.")
- **Benefit Want:** The perception of the benefits the prospect wants to receive in any product or service. ("I want your product to work smoothly so we don't have downtime.")
- **Provider Want:** The characteristics of the ideal service provider a prospect wants to do business with. ("I want you to be more interested in me as a customer than what you're selling.")

- **Price Want:** How the prospect wants to perceive the ideal price. ("I want a price that is justified by the benefits your product provides.")

Your job is to position your presentation specifically for the type of buyer you're approaching, tailoring it to describe and articulate properly each of the buyer's wants before you verbalize them in terms based on needs.

## Why You Must Pay Attention to Needs *and* Wants

The salesperson who understands this has the key to selling: **Decision makers are most eager to buy what they need from salespeople who understand what they want.**

Pay attention to the words "most eager." Sure, lots of times decision makers buy what they need from salespeople who don't have a clue about what they want. Common sense tells you that when the decision maker has a need that absolutely must be satisfied, somebody will get the order—even though not one of the competing salespeople comes within light years of the decision maker's wants. Decision makers aren't very eager about buying in that situation, but they don't have a choice.

You don't want decision makers buying from you for that reason, do you? The idea isn't to force them to settle for doing business with you, but it's to make them *eager* for it. You'll never achieve that in a big way unless you understand that decision makers have wants and needs, emotions and intellect. In other words, you must come face-to-face with the startling fact that decision makers are human beings.

## Who Influences the Buying Decision?

In a large corporation or government agency, buying decisions are most frequently made by some sort of formal or informal committee. The formal structure of the organization is the "official" way the company works; for example, the purchasing department makes purchasing decisions. But there's always an informal structure, no matter how large or small the organization. The informal structure is how the organization really works; for example, the purchasing agent may be strongly influenced by an engineer to purchase a particular technical part, or a midlevel VP to source items from a particular corporate partner.

As you approach a prospective client, it's a good idea for you to determine—at a minimum—who plays each of the following roles in the particular decision-making process to buy or not buy what you sell, keeping in mind that decisions are most often made by consensus.

1. **Buffer:** This is the person whose role is to keep you safely away from the real source of power. It might be a receptionist, a product specialist, or a purchasing agent. It is whomever you perceive to be actively distancing you from the decision-making process.

2. **User:** This is the person who is the beneficiary of the product or service you sell. If you sell bearings, it's the person who's responsible for installing the bearings into the company's product. If you sell accounting software, it's the accounting team members.

3. **Check Writer:** This is literally the person who physically (or electronically) writes the checks to purchase the products or services you provide. The check writer may or may not be the ultimate decision maker.

4. **Internal Advocate:** This is one of the most important people for you to identify as you attempt to enter an account, and he or she will likely give you assistance as you navigate the corporate maze of policies, procedures, and personnel. He or she usually provides subtle (or not-so-subtle) pressure on your behalf. Ideally, you'll have several internal advocates.

At this point, you may be thinking, "Great. Nice info. But now what?" I strongly recommend that you develop an Influence

Map for each company you're selling into (or attempting to sell into). An Influence Map will help you uncover buying patterns, informal decision-making structures, and motives for each individual touch-point you have within the organization.

Here's a sample Influence Map, which I'll explain in the section that follows:

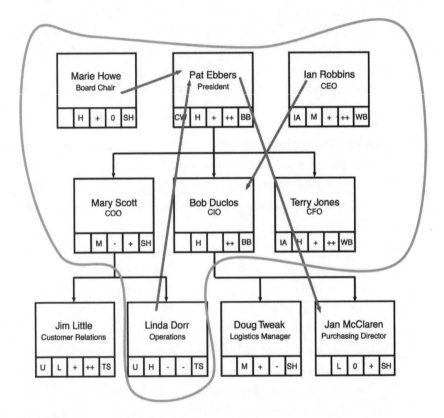

**FIGURE 8.1**   Influence Map

### Here's how to do it:

1. Draw the reporting structure for the organization.

2. Put influencers' names and titles in each box.

3. Draw a line from any person who influences another person to the person (or people) they influence. Don't forget outside influencers!

4. Make note of the role that each plays in the decision-making process: Buffer, User, Internal Advocate, or Check Writer.

5. Describe their level of influence: high, medium, or low.

6. Their preference: favors us, neutral, favors alternative.

7. The quality of contact you have with each person: none, low, good, strong.

8. Your estimate of what drives each person to purchase: price, benefits, unique offering, security, relationships, choice, loyalty, or whatever you believe motivates them. Remember, motivators (*wants*) are different from needs!

Now that we have an Influence Map, what do we do with it? We use it as a map of the organization, reminding us of all the essential contacts we need to make. And we use it to help us craft the messages that make the most lasting impact on each individual we're in contact with. As I've said, what words and messages work best will depend strongly on (a) the individual's organizational role and (b) the individual's role in the specific decision-making process to buy what you sell. How will you know what works? Read on.

## Words That Sell

My late friend and collaborator Tom Travisano observed more than 12,000 pre- and post-sales interactions between salespeople and decision makers over a 20-year period. Together, we began to explore the concept that certain words work with great precision in specific sales situations with varying customer types. We analyzed the motivations of a variety of decision-maker types and produced an extensive library of terms and phrases (known as the Words That Sell) that each responds to most favorably as they relate to the overall sales relationship, perception of products and services, benefits most sought, and expectations of vendor delivery and price. For example, the Words That Sell best for a corporate CEO are not the same Words That Sell best for a midlevel company executive, and those that work best for a purchasing manager are not those that will work most effectively for a technical expert.

In the next few sections, I'm going to describe the Words That Sell to address each of the five wants that have an impact on corporate buyers' decisions for three common buyers with whom you may come into contact: purchasing managers, corporate executives, and facilities managers. These words can be used in direct mail pieces, letters, sales presentations, and anywhere else that you'll be positioning yourself, your company, and your products or services. What's most important, though, is that you pay attention to the reasons behind these word choices—what's motivating the individual in the position not just to make a purchasing decision, but to come to work and perform every day.

## Purchasing Managers

The typical purchasing manager wants to be considered by executive management as being equal to managers in other departments. Often put in the role of the "go-between," they can be unsure about what to buy or the conditions under which to buy it. User groups rarely take the time to inform purchasing agents of anything but the most rudimentary facts. "If it meets the specs, I don't care who you buy it from," is an expression purchasing agents report hearing frequently from their users. What purchasing managers may hear in this expression is: "I made the important decision. Now *you* can make the ***unimportant*** one."

Yet the purchasing manager is in a position of power—because he or she can issue purchase orders. It's absolutely crucial, therefore, that purchasing agents perceive a product or service to be easy to understand. If yours is in fact easy to understand, don't assume you have no challenge here. What your product or service *is* has little to do with how it's *perceived*. Except for the very simplest products and services, a certain degree of education

| | Purchasing Manager | Corporate Executive | Facility Manager |
|---|---|---|---|
| Primary Want | *Initially engage your prospect with words like...* | | |
| | Get recognition | Teamwork | Concrete |
| | Be respected for what you do | Not sticking your neck out | Clear-cut |
| | Get credit | Staying in the mainstream | Tangible |
| | You probably do a lot more than you get credit for | Sensible responsibilities | Real |
| | Gain respect | Be involved in all the important decisions | Real-world |
| | You're doing important work | Insulate yourself | Hands-on |
| | Make a big contribution | Protect yourself from unwarranted intrusions | Perform/Performance |
| | You're important to your company's success | Keep everything on a safe course | |
| Product or Service Want | *Position your product or service with words like...* | | |
| | Easy to understand | Supports what you have already accomplished | Built-in simplicity |
| | A safe purchase | Is not a departure from what you are doing | Easy to figure out |
| | Doesn't require a lot of technical education | Right in line with the direction you are taking | Not rocket science |
| | Not technically challenging | | Easy for people to use |

**FIGURE 8.2** Words That Sell

| | Purchasing Manager | Corporate Executive | Facility Manager |
|---|---|---|---|
| **Benefit Want** | *Position the benefits your product or service offers with words like…* | | |
| | Things should run smoothly for you | Nothing you have to defend or explain | Keep it running |
| | Quietly | Nothing you have to apologize for | Maintain the performance you want |
| | No crises | Results everyone accepts | Keep getting the results you want |
| | Decisions that are certain and sure | The outcome everyone accepts | Consistency |
| **Provider Want** | *Position your organization with words like…* | | |
| | Sincere | Good team players | Regular people |
| | Non-judgmental | Widely accepted | Down to earth |
| | Patient | Blend in well with everyone | Just like you |
| | Not technically obsessed with their product or service | Committed to a team approach | Think the way you do |
| | More interested in their customers than in what they're selling | | Your ideas and opinions matter |
| | Don't attach any strings to a relationship with you | | Straightforward |
| | People | | Nothing slick |
| **Price Want** | | *Position your price with words like…* | |
| | Directly related to the benefits | Priced within the mainstream | Stable |
| | Justified by the benefits | In line with the industry | Not subject to wide swings |
| | Easily translated into the benefits you get | | No radical shifts |

**FIGURE 8.2** Words That Sell (*continued*)

is unavoidable. Purchasing agents know it and accept it. Make certain, therefore, that your product or service is at least *perceived* as not technically challenging or requiring significant education.

Just as your product or service must be perceived as easy to understand and capable of being bought safely without much technical education, you have to be perceived as being not technically obsessed with your product or service. The typical provider can't resist the urge to "educate" purchasing agents about the esoteric complexities of the product or service, and this instruction rarely benefits the decision maker. Salespeople resort to the education tactic whenever they sense a wall of resistance over issues such as price and delivery.

By trumpeting the technical virtues of whatever they're selling, they hope to overcome problems that exist with regard to those other issues. It doesn't work. Worse yet, it aggravates the decision maker's fears about not being knowledgeable enough or respected enough, and it intensifies his or her resistance to making a buying decision. Most purchasing agents want *some* education; however, it has to occur under specific conditions. It must be:

1. In simple terms: It must be expressed in simple and easy-to-grasp terms but not so rudimentary as to be insulting.
2. Not related to sales: The education should never be offered at a time when you're trying to make or save a sale.
3. Gradual: The education must be delivered in small "packets" over an extended span of time. And if you're in doubt, err on the side of making the packet smaller and making the time span longer.
4. Minimal: Don't be overly ambitious. These decision makers have no desire to be technical wizards—they simply want to know enough to avoid embarrassing themselves with glaring mistakes.

Interestingly, it's more common for this decision maker to be recognized for poor—rather than good—performance. Almost every other department shifts accountability for mistakes to the purchasing agent. When a provider doesn't deliver on time, it was the purchasing agent who selected them. A bad purchase, therefore, is never hung on the user's door. It's always dropped right at the feet of the purchasing department.

In other words, success will go unnoticed, but mistakes draw an unbelievable amount of fire. So it's no surprise that purchasing agents require decision-making certainty, because for them, making the right decision ensures that the users will be satisfied. Unfortunately, the users' sense of satisfaction is almost never expressed unless you define "expressed" as "the absence of complaining." No, your product or service won't cause end users suddenly to begin heaping praise on the purchasing department. But what you can hope for—and what the purchasing agent is willing to settle for—is silence from users.

Of all the decision-maker types, purchasing agents probably have the most notorious reputation for price sensitivity. Actually, they care very little about how much you charge for your product or service. It only matters when it becomes a cause of controversy between themselves, their superiors, or the finance department. Purchasing agents will do business with you even if your price is higher than what your competitors are charging—but only if that higher price can be translated into benefits. In other words, the purchasing agent has to be able to say, "Even though they charge more, I still chose them because. . . ."

## Corporate Executives

You may find that it takes months just to get an appointment with a corporate executive. Because of that, it's easy to make the mistake of concluding he or she is a tough sell whose schedule is crammed with important meetings and other monumentally important events. But the real reason these decision makers can be so inaccessible has nothing to do with their workloads and everything to do with their need for insulation. The fact is, they are nervous about letting outsiders in and will do almost anything to avoid it. Every outsider and every provider they allow in is a reflection on themselves. Corporate executives are sensitive to being embarrassed in front of their coworkers and, at the same time, never want to be forced to defend an unpopular decision—or worse yet, apologize for it.

Corporate executives—midlevel managers, vice presidents, directors, and so on—want to feel like they're an essential part of their organizations, but they don't typically want to be singled out for extraordinary responsibilities. They want to be included in what they perceive to be important processes and decisions, but they're not likely to be willing to rock the boat or spearhead major change.

Radical shifts in direction are simply not a part of this decision maker's universe because they invalidate what has gone on before. Instead, every new purchase must be justified as yet one more complementary step—another building block that fits in neatly with all the previous steps and blocks. Even in those rare situations in which a product or service does represent a substantial departure from past practices, you will find corporate executives concocting all sorts of elaborate reasons for why this is not the case.

An interesting drama takes place when a corporate executive senses he or she has been omitted from an important decision-making process or development project. Deviating from his or her usual cooperative "don't rock the boat" style, the offended party can be a difficult obstacle. Corporate executives are not, in fact, above issuing threats that they will sabotage a project unless they are consulted on it, which certainly is exceptional behavior for someone who wants to be a good team player.

But that is exactly the point. Being excluded from the process is evidence that they are *not* highly regarded team players. Interestingly, many corporate executives will instantly reverse themselves and become supportively cooperative the moment they are included in the process.

There is a huge paradox here: Corporate executives crave anonymity, which causes them to avoid making large numbers of decisions. After all, the fewer decisions you make, the less chance you will stand out in a negative way. Yet because they make so few truly important decisions, each one they do make takes on an exceptional significance for them—merely because it is such a rarity!

This is why salespeople who represent smaller or less well-known companies are so frequently disappointed when corporate executives decide to go with the old tried and true providers with the big names and fabled reputations. Despite what the salespeople might believe, the decision had little to do with features, benefits, prices, or any of the other conventional issues. It was, more often than not, strictly a matter of which provider would have the better chance of being acceptable to everyone who's involved.

**Corporate executives are convinced a provider must pass muster in three corporate directions:**
1. Upward (with superiors)
2. Laterally (with peers)
3. Downward (with subordinates)

Because the team concept is so fundamental to these decision makers, an objection from any of the three directions can kill a potential sale, but a positive reaction from all three directions will put your product or service squarely into the revenue stream along with the "old tried and true." These decision makers can be boundlessly enthusiastic about doing business with you, only to reverse their opinion instantly if they get flack from any of the three directions. Your relationship will only take on a tone of permanence if and when you have established yourself over a very long period of time. Until then, however, you're only as good as the latest opinion rendered by a superior, a peer, or a subordinate. (And by the way, doesn't it make sense that the more points of contact you have in an account, the less likely it will be that any of the team members will be a threat to you?)

Your price must be perceived as being close to your competition's prices. Pricing your product or service substantially higher than your competition's is a recipe for disaster. Not even the most courageous corporate executive—not even the one who is completely enchanted with you—will be able to comfortably pay what could be perceived by others as an inflated price.

## Facility Managers

If you sell to them already, you know that facilities managers are usually hands-on people who have little patience with you if you try to deal in ambiguities. These decision makers tend to mistrust anything that can't be seen or touched. And because they want "concreteness," they believe simplicity is a desirable virtue. I've seen salespeople mistake facilities managers' need for tangible, concrete answers for lack of intelligence; and this is a big mistake.

Facilities managers can and do understand and use very sophisticated products and services, and they feel comfortable doing so. Their concern for simplicity stems from the fact that they are typically very sensitive toward their subordinates. In fact, they're one of the most "paternal" of all managers, regardless of the industry or application, largely because they identify with their subordinates more strongly than with management, even though they're in a management position.

Most of these decision makers are well known for having a very friendly but "no-nonsense" style. You might think that they're "bottom-line" people who like to cut right to the heart of the matter without a lot of talking and speculating. And that's true to a degree, but their attitude in this regard is more indicative of what they consider their own personal weakness in handling certain kinds of interactions skillfully. They feel extremely vulnerable, most uncertain, and most exposed to the perceived dangers of "being sold" when they're in close contact with people who aren't forthright and direct—in other words, people who are persuasive "sales types."

But what if you provided evidence that you respected their opinions? For these decision makers, that would be a welcome change from what they're accustomed to in their world. Facilities managers typically believe they're denied a certain degree of respect by other professionals. In other words, their opinions don't "count as much" as do the ideas and suggestions of many other people, both inside and outside the company.

For most of these decision-makers, accomplishing today what you accomplished yesterday—and achieving tomorrow what you achieved today—is good enough. In other words, the value of consistency is almost unmatched by anything else. Nothing associated with you should be perceived as radical, sudden or unexpected. The "fabric" of the decision-maker's experience with you has to be smooth and seamless. They're looking for a stable price that has never been, nor will be, subject to radical change. If a product or service is genuinely reliable—and if it has an impressive install base—it's obviously a long-term "player" in the market.

## Purchasing Parlance: The Unique Vocabulary of Purchasing

Now that we've looked at the Words That Sell for a few key decision-maker types, let's look at some of the specific terminology that you're likely to see on supplier qualification forms and RFPs and in meetings with corporate buyers. If you've not sold to a corporate buyer before, it can be easy to be surprised by acronyms and purchasing terms that you may not have heard before. But during a sales presentation to corporate purchasing agents, you need to be comfortable using their language, and you should feel comfortable that the buyer isn't going to ask you a question that you can't answer simply because you're unfamiliar with the terminology he or she is using. (To make things even more complicated, terminology will differ from corporation to corporation.)

The list below briefly defines some terms commonly used in purchasing. By the time this book gets published, there will likely be other, newer technology, terminology, and methods that augment these; but this list of the basics should be helpful to you.

- **ABC (activity-based costing):** a methodology that measures the cost and performance of cost objects, activities and resources.

- **CCM (centralized commodity management):** a purchasing program where a commodity manager buys for all plants or divisions regardless of his home base. This eliminates responsibility for commodity purchases by buyers at individual plants and tends to increase contract longevity with the vendor.

- **CPM (certified purchasing manager):** professional designation awarded by the Institute for Supply Management to individuals demonstrating broad experience, competence, and integrity.

- **ERP (enterprise resource planning):** software that coordinates all the resources, information, and activities needed to complete business processes such as order fulfillment or billing. ERP maintains in a single database the data needed for a variety of business functions such as manufacturing, supply chain management, financials, projects, human resources, and customer relationship management.

- **JIT (Just-In-Time):** refers to a program for reducing cost or eliminating waste by assembling only the minimum resources necessary to add value to a product. It is often mistaken as an inventory program because low inventories are one of the essential elements. It is also customer- or sales-focused rather than production-focused.

- **MRO (maintenance, repairs, and overhaul):** purchasing department expenditures for preservation or enhancement of existing capital assets or resources.

- **MRP (manufacturing resource planning):** a systematic approach to purchasing which includes forecasting needs, identifying sources, establishing delivery schedules and monitoring progress.

- **NAICS (North American Industry Classification System):** assigns goods and services a code. Used by the federal government, particularly the Department of Commerce's Bureau of the Census, as well as private industry.

- **PM (purchasing manager):** one who coordinates, directs, and possibly trains buyers and assistant purchasing managers, while maintaining buying responsibilities.

- **SPC (statistical process control):** a quantitative tool for enhancing quality control relying on probability, theory, and random sampling to assure that predetermined standards are maintained.

- **VA (value analysis):** an approach to cost reduction in which components are analyzed to determine whether they can be redesigned, standardized, or made by less costly methods of production.

- **VMI (vendor managed inventory):** the buyer of a product provides information to a vendor of that product, and the vendor takes full responsibility for maintaining an agreed inventory of the material.

Remember, no matter how large a corporation or agency you're trying to sell into, you're selling to individual people with unique wants and needs that (at least on the surface) may seem to have little to do with the purchasing decision you'd like them to make. If you have positioned yourself well and made the effort to communicate with decision makers in the ways that they are most comfortable with, you're ahead of the vast majority of your peers.

## Critical Points from This Chapter

- At the core, you're not selling to a giant corporation. You're selling to an individual or group of individuals who represent the corporation but are motivated by their own unique psychological requirements and professional desires.

- Decision makers' needs and wants depend on many factors, but they're strongly correlated with (a) the role an individual plays within an organization and (b) the position he or she has in the decision-making process to use (or not use) your company's product or service.

- Needs are application related, at the surface, rational, fact-oriented, and product- or service-specific. Wants are personal, below the surface, emotional, perception-oriented, and not product- or service-specific.

- Decision makers are very aware of the direct relationship between their needs and the buying decisions they make. You can't say the same for wants. In our research, we found that decision makers choose to reveal their wants to the salesperson less than 2 percent of the time.

- Decision makers are most eager to buy what they need from salespeople who understand what they—the decision makers—want.

# Developing Your
# Sales Presentation

## Everything Up Until Now Was Prework

You may have noticed that virtually all of the preceding chapters were dedicated to the tremendous amount of work you must do before you ever get in front of a corporate giant or government agency prospect. And you may have figured out the reason why: Nowhere are the "Three Ps" of prospecting, positioning, and precall planning more important than when selling to the giants. Each of these three elements is absolutely essential to (a) getting a face-to-face meeting with a purchasing manager or executive at a huge organization and (b) being seen as credible and qualified once you do get face-to-face.

Having the opportunity to present your firm to a giant is rare enough, and many people destroy their own chances at winning business simply because they bungle it. One of the most critical steps in winning business from corporate giants is meeting face-to-face with the purchasing manager or other corporate executives. At this meeting, you can score big or watch a valuable sales opportunity fall apart.

If you've been granted an informal meeting with a purchasing manager or company executive, your goals are to position yourself and your firm as low-risk, high-benefit resources for the corporate giant. In most cases, your goal should not be to win business immediately; instead, think of this as an exploratory meeting. Your role will be to ask intelligent questions to determine possible areas in which your firm could provide assistance, and to establish your firm as a potential provider. Whether you're dealing with a corporate giant who already uses one of your competitors, or you're hoping to convince the giant to outsource something it's been doing in-house, don't expect immediate gratification. This meeting is about opening doors and making the giant aware that you've got something of great value to offer.

If you're meeting with corporate personnel because you're a "semifinalist" in a request for proposal process, your goal is to make a clear, effective presentation of the solution(s) you've recommended while positioning yourself and your firm as knowledgeable industry experts and strong potential partners for the large corporation. In general, your best approach is to deliver a brief, concise summary of your solution, then have ample time for discussion. In most cases, this is the meeting to which you should bring other company personnel who would be active in providing the solution you're recommending. You want to present your firm as a solid, reliable, effective company that is poised to provide exemplary service to the giant corporation, and having your ducks in a row for this critical presentation will go a long way toward creating that impression.

Regardless of your reason for the sales meeting, there are five elements of calling on corporate purchasers—whether they're purchasing managers or other corporate executives who have the authority to commit to a purchase of the products or services you sell:

1. Preparation
2. Professionalism
3. Presentation
4. Proof
5. Performance

In our IMPACT Selling process, this meeting is most likely the Meet Step, and if you're on track, the Probe Step. It's highly unlikely—but not impossible, of course—that you'll move beyond the Probe Step during this meeting. In fact, the Probe Step may last for months, or even years, with a corporate giant or government agency. This is why it takes patience and resilience to sell to these major organizations. However, if you're reading this book, I'm going to assume that you are willing to stay on track and keep your focus.

## Preparation: Precall Planning

Establishing productive business relationships with new customers can be a challenging task, even if you've completed a prequalification process and even if you've already done business with the organization. The key to effective sales presentations is advance preparation, and you should be extensively prepared for every sales call you make—whether it's with a new prospect or a long-time client. We've talked a lot about precall planning already, but let's take a few minutes to review the essentials.

The first step? Review everything you find about your prospective client, including annual and quarterly corporate reports, product and service pamphlets, supplier guides, other company brochures, and industry information. (Later when making your presentation, you can refer to some of these items directly.) If you have called on a corporation previously, your preparation should obviously include a file review. Your past relationship with a corporation, if any, provides the foundation on which you will build a future contract. From your files you might be reminded:

- how contact with the corporation began,
- to whom your correspondence has been addressed,
- who has responded to your queries, and
- to whom you have spoken on the phone.

Next, identify and define your prospective buyer's needs and wants—to the extent possible—before shaping your presentation. Here are a few questions that spring to mind:

- Is the prospect coming off a profitable quarter and looking to expand?

- Is he or she seeking to reduce inventories and costs?
- Is just-in-time (JIT) delivery preferable?
- What is the buyer's highest priority at this time: Quality upgrades? Low price?
- What motivates this particular buyer to make a purchase?
- Against whom are you competing? What are your competitors' unique strengths and weaknesses?
- What are the corporation's past buying habits? How does this particular person make a buying decision?

Every little bit of information you can gather about the company with which you hope to do business has a part to play. One of my favorite unfortunate stories is about a salesperson I'm going to call Joy to protect her identity. Joy is typically beautifully positioned with her prospects and customers, and she's called on often by her clients to provide insight and meet additional requirements. A few years back, however, Joy got complacent and didn't prospect as much as she had in the past. She had so much repeat business; she got lazy about seeking out new business.

All of a sudden, Joy lost three big accounts. And the main reason she lost them was that one of her competitors got in front of the corporate buyers at the end of the previous budget cycle, helping her (former) clients spread out expenses and improve their inventory processes. Joy's competitors didn't do anything Joy *couldn't* have done—she just *hadn't* done it, so she lost the accounts. I tell this story so often because it perfectly illustrates Napoleon's famous line: "To be outmaneuvered? Yes. To be surprised? Never."

Poor Joy got surprised *and* outmaneuvered! She had all the capabilities she needed, but she wasn't paying attention. And it cost her dearly.

When you make the call to schedule an appointment, remember that you're setting the stage for a face-to-face presentation that can lead to—or continue—a strong business relationship. Remember to use your direct value statement and your statement of intention. Specify the amount of time you would like that buyer to allocate for your presentation, and make it clear that others are welcome to attend your presentation. Some buyers place strict time limitations on appointments and new business presentations.

## Professionalism—and the Importance of the First 19 to 34 Seconds

Most of us have some anxiety before any important appointment we schedule. One of the best ways to calm your fears is to be prepared—which we've already talked about—and to feel in control of the meeting when it does occur. Begin by confirming your appointment one day in advance by telephone. Or, if you have enough advance time, consider a handwritten note or friendly e-mail to remind your contact of your upcoming appointment.

The day before your meeting, perform critical checks. Is your briefcase organized so that you can easily obtain any documents you need? Do you have a notepad or notebook to use for jotting notes during the interview? These notes could later be used when a contract is being prepared.

On meeting day, plan an early arrival to the plant or corporate headquarters. *Arrive at least 20 minutes early.* Use any extra time to collect your thoughts and to review your presentation, and visualize yourself being successful. You have only a few seconds to establish your credibility and persuade the buyer that investing time with you will be worth it. In fact, research shows that people make decisions about one another in the first 19 to 34 seconds of contact! Don't allow the first impression a buyer has of you to be one of a scrambling, chaotic, disorganized person. Get there early and stay in stride.

Enter the meeting with confidence, enthusiasm, and drive, but never overpower a prospect. Remember:

NO UNSOLICITED SMALL TALK. Use your statement of intention: "Thank you for seeing me today. If it's alright with you, I'd like to have the chance to ask you a few questions to see whether we may have something that would be of value to you. If, together, we find that I can't help you, I can certainly recommend someone who can. Does that sound reasonable?"

## Your Presentation

You should always prepare a presentation that will be brief but thorough. If you're presenting your firm's capabilities in an informal meeting, I'd skip the slides entirely and only use sales aids as leave-behinds. Focus on establishing rapport and having an informative, engaging dialogue with the prospect, gathering as much information from them as you can.

If you're presenting a specific solution to a prospect, consider using samples and audiovisual aids such as pictures, videos, and Web sites, or a simple slide presentation. The key words with all of your presentation materials are "simple and professional." Most salespeople use far too many slides in slide presentations, and they basically read the slides to their prospects. You should have minimal slides—we like to say no more than 10 for a 45-minute presentation—with as few words as possible on them. The slide content should be complementary to what you're saying, not a replacement for your own knowledge.

Of course, the buyer's primary interest will be on how you can fulfill his or her buying needs. Because the buyer-supplier relationship is looked on as a partnership—out of necessity, including discussion of a long-term relationship and disclosure of sensitive information about one another's operations—demonstrate that you are a supplier of reputation. Your chief task is to leave no doubt in the purchasing manager's mind that you can deliver on time and within the quality parameters he or she requires.

I can't emphasize enough the importance of keeping your focus on your prospect during your meeting. Yes, you are there to begin the process of convincing the company or government agency to choose you as a supplier, and you certainly should be prepared to present your qualifications. But asking intelligent questions and really listening to your prospect's responses should be your two primary goals.

---

**Here's a checklist to ensure that you deliver a superior performance during your presentation:**

*Be clear about your objectives.* Are you trying to close a sale on a specific item on this initial call, or are you seeking to make a contact and crystallize the buyer's needs?

*Develop a statement of intention based on your objectives.*

*Articulate the potential matches* between the buyer's needs and your goods and services. Be precise and clear about these matches.

*Emphasize quality* in your presentation. Generally speaking, quality goods and services are the highest priorities for purchasing managers. Give specific examples of your quality control procedures. Show how quality control results in reduced waste.

*Focus on dependability.* Emphasize your commitment to timely and reliable delivery. Describe your warranty and liability protection benefits, if any.

*(continued)*

---

(*continued*)

*Highlight cost-competitiveness.* Be prepared to justify your costs and the prices you charge with specific data. A simple cost-value analysis on previous jobs should reveal cost-cutting factors and demonstrate your ability to minimize waste and rework. Gauge whether the buyer is merely seeking bid quotes for a pricing decision or is exploring other purchasing issues as well.

*Be specific about your contracting procedures.* Include a sample of your standard sales agreement, if appropriate.

*Use visuals and other materials* to support your oral presentation. For example, graphs are an effective way to illustrate growth in sales revenues or increased production performance. However, there is no need to go overboard on audiovisuals. Keep it simple!

*Be positive, enthusiastic, and responsive* to the customer's wishes during the presentation. Be sensitive to the buyer's needs at all times; don't waste his or her time on topics about which no interest is indicated. Be prepared to answer questions during your presentation. Solicit additional questions at the end of your prepared remarks.

*If possible, bring along one or two of your key employees* who would be working on the prospective customer's account. They can answer specific questions and help establish the rapport necessary for good customer relations.

*Conclude your presentation by establishing the steps for future action.* Will you get a price quotation to the buyer by a specific date? Will you invite the buyer to tour your facility? Or will you call within a week to follow up the presentation? The mark of super sellers is follow up; the mark of the majority of would-be suppliers is lack of follow-up.

The first impression you create is critical. Unless corporate buyers are impressed with you personally and with the company you represent, they may never follow up the presentation with further qualification activities. As a result, they may never find out what a good product or service your company can deliver.

## Questions for Senior-Level Decision Makers

Over the years, we've developed a list of questions that we call Silver Bullet Questions: They're all-purpose inquires that will help you elicit valuable information from your prospects and position you as a strategic thinker and problem solver. As salespeople on our team have used these questions and trained other companies' salespeople to use them, we've refined a group of these questions that seem to be most effective with senior-level decision makers.

Please note that this is not a rote checklist that you should run through any time you have a meeting with a prospect or client. Instead, think of these questions as samples or guidelines for the *type* of issues you should be discussing with your contacts. You may not ever cover all of the questions in one meeting—or even most of them. In fact, one single question could form the basis of an entire conversation.

When you ask decision makers questions like these, you'll be amazed at the response you get and the level of rapport you build with them, especially if you're able to build on their responses to lead the discussion toward potential applications for your products or services.

### High-Level Silver Bullet Questions

- What are the top five challenges your organization faces today? How are you addressing those challenges? If these five challenges remain unaddressed, what is the likely outcome?

- What do you believe are your organization's core strengths, weaknesses, opportunities, and threats?

- Where do you see your organization relative to the competition today? Whom do you view as the competition? Are there any emerging, nontraditional competitive threats?

- Does your organization plan to grow? If so, will it be through organic growth or acquisitions? What are the implications of merging with acquired companies?

- How does your long-term vision differ from how your organization is today?

- Over the past 18 to 24 months, what have been your organization's biggest challenges?

- Could you tell me more than I currently know about your customer base? How, if at all, is it changing?

- Have you identified other value-added sources for gaining additional revenue from your existing customers or expanding into new markets with new applications or services?

- What do you believe is the relative value that your customers get from doing business with your organization versus your competition's?

- How can we help you advance your business plan?

- What would you like for us to do for you that we are not currently doing?

## How Decision Makers Perceive *You*

Over the years of firsthand observation, research, and client interaction, we've seen a lot of what works (and doesn't work) with key decision makers at all types of organizations. From large to small, for-profit to not-for-profit, there is clear consensus: The salespeople and executives who win the most business, at the highest margins, are perceived as strategic resources who add value far beyond selling a part or service.

| If you come across as a . . . | Product Salesperson | Business Expert | Strategic Resource |
|---|---|---|---|
| **Their impression of you will be . . .** | You're a product pusher. | You're a potential resource. | You're a trusted advisor. |
| **Their impression of your sales call will be . . .** | It's an interruption. | It's a sales presentation. | It's a business meeting. |
| **Their conclusion about you will be . . .** | You'll give them some basic product information. | You'll explore creative ideas. | You'll bring compelling value. |
| **The likely outcome will be . . .** | You'll be delegated to a lower level. | You'll be considered. | You'll get continued access to key decision makers. |

As you can see, simply being knowledgeable about your own products or services and your own industry is just not enough. Sure, you need to know your products or services inside and out and be able to answer any question that's thrown at you. But sales—especially to giant corporations—is about far more than passing a product knowledge quiz. You need to be mentally flexible about finding ways to apply your solutions. In many of our sales training programs, we talk about earning "industry expert" status: Being so broadly and deeply knowledgeable about the primary industry (industries) you serve that you are perceived by your prospects and clients as an expert on their line of business.

Becoming an industry expert is a start, but the more I've thought about it, I've realized selling to the giants requires even more than that. (In fact, I think that selling to top-level executives in companies of any size takes more than industry expertise.) The strongest salespeople I've learned from in my life weren't just savvy at selling, or knowledgeable about the businesses they sell into—they were absolutely committed to constantly improving their knowledge about business in general. They are the men and women who are able to think strategically—enabling them to anticipate long-term consequences of today's actions and to uncover solutions that are remedies to significant business challenges for their clients. They don't just sell a part or a service, they see what they are offering as an integral part of their clients' business plans.

## Proof

After you've presented your capabilities and any specific recommendations you have for the buyer, it's time to offer third-party proof of your claims. Although only a few words are necessary in regard to proof, they are important ones. During your meeting with the purchasing manager, you must be prepared to document your company's ability to produce. A brochure, folder, or capability statement that describes what you can do is helpful and can be bolstered by the following:

- letters of recommendation and testimonials,
- references,
- notices of certification, and
- copies of recent awards.

Now, many salespeople make the mistake of offering testimonials, certifications, and so on in the initial stages of the sales call, believing that these materials will enhance their credibility. Interestingly, we've found that this documentation is much more effective when used in what we call the "Convince" step of the sale—after presenting your recommendations and before asking for an order or commitment. Testimonials and other third-party proof used at this point solidify the buyer's impressions of you and make them even more receptive to placing an order with you. Some of the ways the tools can help you include:

- proving your claims,
- bringing witnesses,
- justifying your price, and
- relieving their fear of buying.

## Performance

The fifth "P," performance, relates not only to how you fulfill your contract, but also how you perform before the contract is drawn up. The notes you took during your meeting form the base of the outline for your follow-up letter. The letter should

- review important points covered during the meeting,
- provide answers to any questions that required research, and
- confirm actions that were agreed on.

When the buyer receives your letter, he will remember the meeting and recognize that you are someone who follows through on details. Never promise more than you can deliver. If a purchasing agent begins to expect more than your company is capable of doing, let the truth be known; maintain your integrity. It is better to promise and deliver on a small or medium order than to overpromise on a large one and ruin your firm's reputation. You could lose a repeat customer as well.

## A Word About Team Selling

If you've responded to any requests for proposals (RFPs), you know that a typical solicitation asks you to describe not just a primary point of contact for the client, but also the team that will be responsible for servicing the contract. Particularly with large-scale contracts, no one expects one person to single-handedly sell, service, and support the project—and this is where a trustworthy, intelligent, dedicated team comes into play. Even if you are in the prequalification stages of working with a giant corporation or government agency, there are times that including a small, well-chosen team of employees from your firm in meetings and conference calls will serve you well.

### Team selling is all about:

- Assembling a group of experts who stand ready to provide excellent service and support to your potential client.
- Letting subject-matter experts—engineers, accountants, trainers, operations managers, and so on—address questions that fall within their areas of expertise.
- Representing your firm as a well-established organization with depth and breadth of capabilities.
- Giving your prospective client multiple resources within your firm.
- Demonstrating that you function well as a team.

In many cases, it is perfectly appropriate—and even desirable—for you to take a "team-selling" approach when selling to large corporations and government agencies. Often, you'll find that corporate buyers use a "team-buying" approach when interacting with you, too. Involving key members of your team in the sales process, when done well, can reduce confusion, ensure reasonable pricing, and make a strong positive impression on your potential client.

On the basis of our deliverables and the positioning of our firm as a sales training vendor, one of our strongest selling points at The Brooks Group is that we have an on-staff curriculum design team and the ability to customize training programs for our clients rapidly and cost-effectively. The vast majority of our best, most loyal clients have benefited from this service, and it's a differentiator for us in the marketplace. So when we've submitted a proposal to a large company and won the opportunity to give a presentation of our solutions, does the salesperson fly solo to the sales meeting? Of course not.

In the best case, we invite our prospect to visit our facility—our well-outfitted training center and dedicated staff position us well and ensure that we're perceived as low-risk and poised to respond quickly to client requirements. In some cases, of course, we have to travel to our prospects' location to deliver our presentation, but in either case, we showcase the strength and depth of our team. Typically, we'll ensure that the prospective client interacts with our curriculum design expert, the facilitator who would oversee the training effort for their organization, and the assessment manager who would be managing the assessments they'd use.

In most cases, the salesperson who's hosting the prospect at The Brooks Group also will encourage the senior-most member of the prospect's team to spend some time with one or more of our more seasoned consultants—whether one-on-one or as part of a group event. There are times in a complex sale when bringing in your firm's CEO or president (if that's not you) can play a pivotal part in earning a contract with a giant corporation.

Whatever product or service you sell, it's usually a good idea to get your team involved in the sales process wherever possible. If you have impressive facilities, make every effort to get your prospects to visit your locale. Showing the giants that you have solid capabilities and an established infrastructure will help combat any lingering fears they may have that you might be a "high-risk" vendor.

In the next chapter, I'll talk all about being a successful bidder and negotiating contracts, which can be lengthy and difficult processes.

## Critical Points from This Chapter

- Each of the "Three Ps"—prospecting, positioning, and pre-call planning—are absolutely essential to (a) getting a face-to-face meeting with a purchasing manager or executive at a huge organization and (b) being seen as credible and qualified once you do get face-to-face.

- Five key elements of calling on corporate purchasers:
  1. Preparation
  2. Professionalism
  3. Presentation
  4. Proof
  5. Performance

- If you're presenting your firm's capabilities in an informal meeting, I'd skip the slides entirely and use only sales aids as leave-behinds. If you're presenting a specific solution, consider using samples and audio-visual aids such as pictures, videos, and Web sites, or a simple slide presentation (no more than 10 slides for a 45-minute presentation!).

- Your chief task is to leave no doubt in the purchasing manager's mind that you can deliver on time and within the quality parameters he or she requires.

- Silver Bullet Questions will help you elicit valuable information from your prospects and position you as a strategic thinker and problem solver.

- From large to small, for-profit to not-for-profit, there is clear consensus: The salespeople and executives who win the most business, at the highest margins, are perceived as strategic resources who add value far beyond selling a part or service.

- The strongest salespeople aren't just savvy at selling, or knowledgeable about the businesses they sell into—they are absolutely committed to constantly improving their knowledge about business in general. They don't just sell a part or service, they see what they are offering as an integral part of their clients' business plans.

- Testimonials, certifications, and so on are more effective when presented AFTER presenting your recommendations (before asking for an order or commitment) than they are when used in the initial stages of the sales process.

- It is better to promise and deliver on a small or medium order than to overpromise on a large one and ruin your firm's reputation.

- Many times, including a small, well-chosen team of employees from your firm in meetings or conference calls will serve you well and position your company as a least-risk vendor. It can reduce confusion and ensure reasonable pricing as well.

# Making a Successful Bid

When you submit a bid to a corporate or government buyer, you'll be in competition with other vendors seeking the same contract. It follows that your bid must be superior—you must go beyond the standard requirements and have the extra edge that will set you apart. My fundamental guidance on bidding is to promise the highest quality product that *you can realistically deliver* using current employees and equipment.

If the buyer has issued specification requirements in an RFI, RFP, or RFQ, make sure you can equal or exceed them. Then, accurately assess your scheduling and delivery abilities. Don't promise what you can't deliver in an attempt to secure the contract. This is all too often the quickest route to failure. Odds are, you'll be stretching your resources so thin to fulfill the contract that you end up barely breaking even. A million-dollar contract *can* actually result in less money in your pocket than a $400,000 one.

Only you can know for sure what's realistic and fiscally responsible for your firm. I strongly encourage you to think about those issues when you are preparing a bid for a large contract. It may save you money, time, personnel morale, and countless headaches. Remember: Not every company is set up to do business with the giants. And even if you *are*, not every contract is (or should be) a winnable one for you.

## He Who Writes the Specs Gets the Checks

Let me bring up one important point here. Have you heard the statement: "He who writes the specs gets the checks?" It is certainly possible to win business from a giant corporation without being involved in writing the specifications. But I submit to you that if you've positioned yourself as a strategic resource and trusted advisor for key decision makers, your ideas and input will be used in developing specifications, whether directly or indirectly. And that's a good thing.

A few years ago, we received an RFP from a large corporation. Initially, we weren't sure why we'd received it, but we discovered that a gentleman who had attended one of our IMPACT Selling programs while working for another organization had since moved on to the RFP-issuing company and been promoted to the upper echelons of the firm. Our program had made such an impression on him, and apparently such a difference in his selling career, that many years later, when he needed to source a sales training firm, we sprang to mind.

Think about it. Everything this man had learned in our program had informed his sales career from that point on. Everything he believed about success at sales had been shaped—at least to some extent—by what we taught him and encouraged in him. Even when he wasn't conscious of it, The Brooks Group's ideas and philosophies were at work in his life. We saw dramatic proof of that when we reviewed the RFP carefully and discovered that many of the requirements discussed in the document were described almost exactly as we would have described them ourselves.

He didn't write the RFP to guarantee we'd win the business. He was conscientious about his job and wanted to evaluate all of his options; after all, it had been many years since he'd dealt directly with The Brooks Group. But luckily for us, we've maintained our approach and continued developing outstanding sales and sales management training programs that fit his company's requirements exactly. As I'm sure you've guessed by now, we won the contract.

**In truth, a combination of factors went into our winning that piece of business:**

- Luck. It was our good luck that a satisfied customer who grew into a decision making position remembered us years later.
- Excellent Service. We delivered on our promise to help make that salesperson a better one when he attended our IMPACT Selling program those years ago.

- Attention to Detail. We reviewed the RFP carefully and only bid on it when we were sure we could meet and exceed its requirements.
- Fair Pricing. We most likely weren't the lowest price, but we offered the company a price that was perceived as fair given the value we demonstrated we could provide.

It's this last point that causes many small firms to go broke. I'm not exaggerating, either. It's incredibly common for small businesses to fall for the "I can cut price if I make it up in volume" fallacy, and it will put you right out of business if you can't get comfortable pricing your offerings and sticking to your prices.

## What's Your Unit Break-Even Point?

Many, many small business owners and salespeople are tempted to underprice their products or services either because they have not properly computed internal costs or they have hopes of winning the contract to get a "foot in the door." Either reason for underbidding is dangerous and may lead to disastrous results, including offering lower quality than agreed on, slower delivery, and customer dissatisfaction. Low bidding can wreak havoc on your cash flow, necessitate refinancing, and yield poor profits. And your client will not be the only party dissatisfied. Low bidding tends to affect your own employees in terms of low morale, loss of confidence, and perhaps burnout because they'll feel they're working twice as hard for less business and as if their hard work is undervalued by company management and salespeople.

It is hard to tell you not to take some marginal jobs, especially when your plant or office is underutilized, you have payroll to meet, or you "just know" that this contract will lead to great things. But let me tell you, even if lower price does win you an order, it will cost you in the long run. Remember, the thing that will give you the upper hand against your competitors is rarely price. It's almost always quality, delivery, service, or some other differentiator you've positioned effectively.

The best way to estimate a fair and competitive price that will yield a profit is to perform a break-even analysis. Here's how:

1. Determine what your fixed costs are. Fixed costs generally do not vary with changes in the number of units produced or sold. The cost of renting your premises, for example, does not change because your production doubles. Rent may increase over time, but not because you're producing more.

2. Determine your variable costs. Variable costs change directly with changes in the number of units you produce or sell. Variable costs per unit are constant; that is, twice as many workers and twice as much material produce twice as much product X.

3. Add your fixed costs to your variable costs to get your total cost.

4. Figure out what your total revenue is by multiplying price times quantity. If you sell 10,000 units of X at $10, your total revenue is $100,000.

5. Subtract total cost from total revenue to get the amount of your profits.

Knowing the number of units you need to sell to break even is important in setting the price. If you find that a product priced at $100 per unit has a variable cost of $60 per unit, then the contribution per unit to fixed costs is $40. With total fixed costs of $120,000, your break-even point in units is determined as follows:

$$\text{Break-even point} = \text{fixed costs/per unit contribution to fixed costs}$$

Using the example above to calculate the break-even point, you'll see:

Break-even point = \$120,000/\$40 per unit = 3,000 units

So, with a \$40 per unit contribution to fixed costs (hence a \$40 gross profit margin per unit), you must sell 3,000 units to break even. Above the break-even point of 3,000 units, in this example, the per unit contribution to fixed costs goes to profits. For example, if you sell 3,001 units, profit equals \$40. Each additional unit that you sell, above 3,000 units, adds another \$40 to your profits.

To calculate your break-even point in terms of dollar sales volume, multiply your break-even point in units by the price per unit. In the earlier example, the break-even point in terms of dollar sales volume would be 3,000 (units) times \$100, which equals \$300,000.

3,000 units × \$100 per unit = \$300,000 break-even point
in sales volume

## Service Provision and Other Safeguards

Your bid price should also take into consideration the cost of providing service. If you can guarantee your service in your bid, that's a big plus. In recent years, product liability has become a major legal issue. The manufacturer of a component part as well as the end manufacturers can be sued. So, state right in your bid whether you will assume responsibility for product liability. (If you do, be sure that your insurance covers it.)

**Avoiding the Midproject Slump:** You score points if, somewhere in your bid, you assure that your firm maintains a continuous or increasing level of performance. When you achieve at least a moderate level of success, problems may occur if you let down your guard. You work hard to win new customers, and you work hard to maintain them. Avoiding the midproject slump is a taxing but rewarding experience because this often means you've successfully avoided the project deadline crunch.

**Don't Underestimate Your Need for Legal Assistance:** All of the giants to whom you'd like to sell employ full-time legal specialists, and many maintain elaborately layered legal departments. There will be times when you should use an attorney skilled in general contract and business law, more so with increasing revenues. Contacting an attorney *before* a contract or bid is signed can prevent problems.

## Preparing the Bid or RFP/RFQ Response

Most giant firms and virtually all government agencies follow standard procedures for acquiring and evaluating competitive bids for products and services they need. Your cooperation in providing responses to their inquiries *in the manner and format in which they are requested* is essential to being taken seriously and having your offering considered as a valuable solution. Many times, the decision maker is literally making a grid of supplier responses to key questions in an RFP or RFQ—they want to be able to compare apples to apples.

In many cases, you'll be asked to provide your pricing details in a precise grid format specified by the RFP or RFQ issuer. I have to be honest—I hate this part of RFPs and RFQs. For us, there are so many variables that go into pricing, and a shift in any one of them can make a huge impact on the bottom-line price. Forcing me to describe one "be all, end all" price goes against everything I believe about sales. My goal is never to be the cheapest provider but to be the one that provides the most value for every dollar my clients invest in The Brooks Group.

So to encourage prospective customers to engage in dialogue with us about their investment, I'll follow the rules, using the standard required format, but I'll provide several alternative pricing scenarios, along the lines of the "good, better, best" solutions you see often in the retail world. Often, this helps focus the RFP issuer on exactly what their requirements are, beyond "lowest price." They may see things in our "best" pricing option that they want, but discover they're willing to let go of a few things that were in the "good" option. I'm often willing to "negotiate" my price, but it usually requires the client to give a little, too, whether it's a monthly volume commitment, more favorable payment terms, or simply leaving out a few items or services that they see as nonessential.

Let's look at this another way by exploring how we recommend presenting price when the format is not specified by RFP/RFQ requirements: We use the Stacking Formula. The idea here is that as the perceived value goes up, the perception of the price goes down. The more someone thinks he or she is getting for the dollars invested, the lower the price will seem.

Here's an example of how we'd present price using the Stacking Formula:

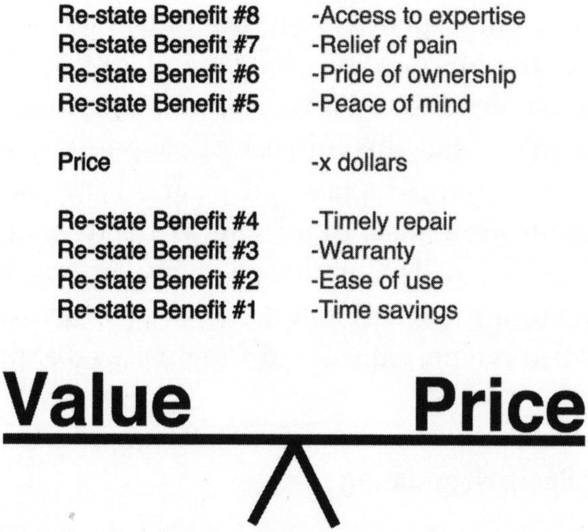

| | |
|---|---|
| Re-state Benefit #8 | -Access to expertise |
| Re-state Benefit #7 | -Relief of pain |
| Re-state Benefit #6 | -Pride of ownership |
| Re-state Benefit #5 | -Peace of mind |
| | |
| Price | -x dollars |
| | |
| Re-state Benefit #4 | -Timely repair |
| Re-state Benefit #3 | -Warranty |
| Re-state Benefit #2 | -Ease of use |
| Re-state Benefit #1 | -Time savings |

**Value** ⟍⟍⟍⟍⟍ **Price**

**FIGURE 10.1**  Stacking

"We understand that you're interested in 24/7 service availability, a 99.8 percent on-time delivery guarantee, and a commitment to innovation. You'll get all of that for an investment of $182 per piece shipped, plus a four-year warranty for all parts, access to our real-time inventory management solution, and a dedicated account representative."

Another valuable tool in your arsenal is a well-crafted, concise cover letter. If you are constrained by a RFP or RFQ response template, the cover letter can be the place to draw attention to what you believe are your main differentiators and the ways that you understand the prospect's requirements.

## All Contracts Are Negotiable

Between the time when you make a bid (or request to bid) on a contract with a major corporation or government agency and the time you actually *win* the contract award, a substantial amount of negotiating is likely to occur. A colleague in the third-party logistics business just told me that while the time from issuance of RFP to submission due date keeps getting shorter, the amount of time spent on clarification, team meetings, and contract negotiations is getting longer and longer. His proposal teams are often required to gather RFP responses together within one or two weeks, but this initial RFP response is followed by months—and sometimes years—of delays, back-and-forth discussions, and negotiations. In the end, virtually all contracts are negotiated in face-to-face exchanges between buyers and sellers; discussion of the terms and methods by which the contract will be fulfilled is a prerequisite to a mutually favorable business transaction.

### Before You Begin Negotiating

The initial—and probably most important—step in becoming a skilled negotiator is to do your homework. Top negotiators agree that the best negotiators are well prepared and have done the following before ever entering into a formal negotiation process:

- **Establish your objectives.** Why are you seeking a particular contract? The answer may seem obvious, but ask yourself this question anyway. Will your bid price produce a profit for your company? How will you meet or exceed contract requirements? Being prepared to answer these questions is essential, for you are likely to be asked questions like these in the process of calling on and selling to the corporate giants.

- **Examine your capabilities.** For example, what advantages do you have over your competitors, particularly in the areas of technology, production, manufacturing, scheduling, or other performance factors? What are your financial needs to complete this contract? Will you seek assistance from the buyer, or can you carry all costs internally? What are your cash flow requirements for the duration of the contract?

- **Determine (in advance) what you really want to get from the negotiation and for what you will settle.** Purchasing agents are more receptive now than ever before to your ideas on improving their operations. Your good ideas are valuable negotiating tools. In many ways, negotiation is like a poker game in that you don't really reveal the cards until after you have won. When you first start negotiating, it is not wise to reveal the exact terms that you want. At the beginning of a negotiation, both the buyer and seller typically will state what they are seeking, and usually these positions seem unreasonable to one another. Throughout the course of the negotiation, each side will make counterproposals and concessions until, hopefully, mutually agreeable positions are reached. Ask for more up front, recognizing that the resulting compromises will eventually come closer to your initial unrevealed position.

- **Anticipate potential negative outcomes and plan your counterproposal.** Most entrepreneurs and salespeople don't have the foresight to do this. During negotiations it may be difficult to accurately assess the impact of suggested positions. If you can anticipate these before negotiating, you won't be surprised by any pushback, and you'll be much more equipped to make alternative suggestions that are more favorable to you.

## Tactical Decision: Individual or Team Negotiations

Effective negotiators also make an important tactical decision before entering into the negotiation process. Will you negotiate as an individual, or will you use a team? This will depend largely on the importance of the negotiation, the time available, and the skills required to successfully close the deal. When selecting a negotiating team, be certain that each member has a specific function. Each person should know the agreed-on strategy and objectives, have a specialty, and be able to demonstrate his or her confidence. Everyone is there to be a productive member of the negotiating team; clear up any internal disagreements you might have well in advance of the negotiation.

**Team negotiation can be very effective; however, using a single negotiator:**

- prevents a "divide and conquer" strategy by opponents,
- demonstrates that you have complete responsibility and authority,
- eliminates a weakening position resulting from differences of opinion among team members, and
- facilitates on-the-spot decision making, particularly in the area of granting or receiving concessions.

## Listen and Rebut

Corporate purchasing agents negotiate far more often than you do, with greater results. If they're part of a top purchasing department, they've received top training. I guarantee you that the number one thing taught in any purchasing training seminar is this: Always challenge the seller's price. Always. No exceptions. It doesn't make any difference what it is you're buying.

If they don't challenge you directly on price, they'll ask you to make a change to your service plan, guarantee faster delivery, or make some other concession that benefits them. If you're not aware of these types of tactics, you are likely to buckle on your price or on some other major provision perhaps only moments before you were about to get what you asked for. Just because a person asks you for a discount or insists on an upgrade from you, it doesn't mean you're doing something wrong. Smart, seasoned, or strong prospects and customers are going to hammer you, even if you make no mistakes as a salesperson. It's just not that easy to avoid. They do it because they've been trained to do it and often are evaluated on the concessions they get.

Remember: Most buyers aren't buying solely on lowest price, even if they say they are. Most buyers are looking for the fairest price, the price that offers the most perceived benefits for the dollar.

The best negotiators listen carefully, calmly, and respectfully to the points presented by the other side. Then they discuss those points, carefully noting which points on which they agree and giving their rationale for disagreeing with any items they have issue with. For example, you might say something like, "We're in agreement that part #A098 is the right choice here, and we're comfortable with accepting responsibility for inventorying three months' of the part in our warehouses. However, we are uncomfortable with taking on responsibility for modeling your inventory needs when we don't have access to your complete strategic plan and previous years' data."

Then, you would follow up with an alternate recommendation that is more suitable in your view. For example, "If we're going to take on inventory of the part, we would prefer that an interagency team collaborate on inventory projections and meet quarterly to review and update their projections."

## Avoiding Big Tactical Mistakes

Selling to large organizations is complicated. There are many critical points in the sales process, and it's likely that you've made tactical mistakes in the past. The following is a list of common tactical errors we see small businesses make, plus suggestions on how to avoid them:

**Mistake #1: Failure to read with meticulous care the solicitation, its attachments, and its specifications.**

There's no question about it. You should read all materials contained in a request for proposal or solicitation. It's also helpful to maintain familiarity with purchasing and procurement procedures, specifications, material allocation, delivery and supply expectations, and related matters.

**Mistake #2: Having inadequate contract administration resources.**

You should obtain appropriate counsel when needed, for advice on matters of bidder's rights and obligations, appeal procedures, termination, and default actions. Be cognizant of the resources required for contract administration and the extensive documentation necessary to manage contracts successfully.

## Self-Analysis:

*WHY DIDN'T WE GET THE JOB?*

**When you visited a prospect, were you and your salespeople:**

- Prepared? Knowledgeable of the customer's needs?
- Knowledgeable of your product or service?
- Dealing with the "right" person?
- Capable of successfully completing the job you were seeking?

**Were you available when your customer tried to reach you:**

- Did you return his or her calls promptly?
- Did you keep the customer informed of progress and problems?
- Did you deliver on time?
- Were your reports comprehensive and well-prepared?

**Consider the impression a visitor has of your office or plant:**

- Is it clean?
- Are supplies stored conveniently yet out of the way?
- Do your employees conduct themselves as "professionals?"
- Would a fresh painting or cleaning improve it?

**Remember: First impressions are lasting impressions.**

**If too many defects caused a problem on previous contracts, examine all of the following areas to identify the problem, correct it, and prevent future problems:**

- Were defects caused by human or machine error?
- How do you handle the responsibility for defects?
  - Don't assign blame.
  - Give authority to deal with the problem.
- What is your frequency rate—the total number of defects compared with total number produced?
- Does your quality-control program prevent defective items from leaving your shop? If not, what can you do to prevent this problem?
- Did you tell the customer your corrective actions?

*(continued)*

*(continued)*

**With hidden and underlying problems, you must "look in the mirror" and be honest with yourself. Was the problem:**

- Yourself—trying to do too much yourself
  - Working 16-hour days, not delegating to others?
  - Were you "on top" of this job or busy doing other things?
- Your employees
- Your equipment—wrong for the job
- Your schedule—unreasonable, and impossible

**Mistake #3: Being excessively optimistic in assessing the task, the risk, and in-house capabilities.**

I can't emphasize enough how critical it is that you take a realistic approach to determining whether your firm has the overall capability, both technical and financial, to perform on selected projects. Delay in receipt of goods and supplies from subcontractors, for example, could cause considerable setbacks during contract performance. Take these factors into consideration when preparing bids and upon contract awards in reviewing the project plan. Approach each solicitation critically and proceed only after generating substantial evidence that you can successfully execute the contract.

**Mistake #4: Bidding on unreliable purchase descriptions or specifications.**

Call or write for clarifications of unclear purchase or specification information. It's worth double-checking, too, to ensure that you've obtained any and all copies of the latest revisions to specifications before submitting a bid.

## Mistake #5: Bidding based on estimations, not factual cost data.

Many firms make the big mistake of preparing cost estimates based on what they think will get them the job. To protect yourself, make your cost estimates on a per-bid basis, neither relying on previously prepared bids nor assuming that standard cost estimates or "ballpark" figures will be sufficient. Key factors should include:

- Subcontractor and equipment vendor costs
- Overhead and overhead rates
- Learning curves for labor and salaried personnel
- Estimate of person-days required
- Availability of government furnished materials and equipment
- Labor and salary rates and predictable changes
- Profit potential

## Mistake #6: Bidding under too much time pressure.

We've discovered that there's often an inverse relationship between how quickly someone wants a proposal and how likely we are to win it. Of course, there are exceptions. But all too often, we've put together a solid proposal on a tight deadline, only to discover later that the company just needed (a) a sanity check before they went with their first choice or (b) ideas for doing their own implementation or something else unrelated to our specific solutions. I'd strongly recommend *not* bidding on even very attractive solicitations when the deadline is not sufficient to prepare a thoroughly researched, double-checked bid.

**Mistake #7: Accepting an unrealistic delivery time frame.**

It's really of no value to you or your firm, in terms of cost, experience, or reputation, to bid on projects when you know in advance that the delivery time frame is unrealistic.

## Critical Points from This Chapter

- Fundamental bidding guidance: Promise the highest-quality product that you *realistically can deliver using current employees and equipment.*

- If you've positioned yourself as a strategic resource and trusted advisor for key decision makers, your ideas and input will be used in developing specifications, whether directly or indirectly. And that's a good thing.

- Many, many small businesses underprice their products or services, either because they have not properly computed internal costs or they have hopes of winning the contract to get a "foot in the door." Either reason for underbidding is dangerous and may lead to disastrous results, including offering lower quality than agreed on, slower delivery, and customer dissatisfaction, as well as cash flow problems, poor profits, and employee morale issues.

- Your break-even point is determined by dividing your fixed costs by the per unit contribution to those fixed costs. Once you know your break-even point, you can calculate it in terms of dollar sales volume.

- Your cooperation in providing responses to prospects' RFPs and RFQs in the manner and format in which they are requested is essential to being taken seriously and having your offering considered as a valuable solution.

- To encourage prospective customers to engage in dialogue with you about their investment, follow the rules, using the standard required format, but consider providing several alternative pricing scenarios.

- If you are constrained by a RFP or RFQ response template, a well-crafted, concise cover letter can be the perfect place to draw attention to what you believe are your main differentiators and the ways that you understand the prospect's requirements.

- Although the time from issue of RFP to submission due date keeps getting shorter and shorter, the time spent on clarification, team meetings, and contract negotiations is getting longer and longer.

- Keys to successful negotiations:
  - Establish your objectives.
  - Examine your capabilities realistically.
  - Determine in advance what you really want to get from the negotiation and for what you will settle.
  - Anticipate potential negative outcomes and plan your counterproposal.

- Just because someone asks you for a discount or insists on an upgrade doesn't mean you're doing something wrong. Smart, seasoned, or strong prospects and customers are going to hammer you, even if you make no mistakes as a salesperson. They do it because they've been trained to do it and often are evaluated on the concessions they get.

- Remember: Most buyers are looking for the fairest price, the one that offers the most perceived benefits for the dollar.

# You've Won It, Now Build On It

Life is good—you've won a contract from a corporate giant and you've negotiated its terms successfully. In all likelihood, this opportunity will transform your business in more ways than you can imagine. If you make the most of it, this can be the best opportunity you've ever seen—but if you bungle it, it can be the biggest headache and wasted investment you've ever faced. Once you've gotten commitment from your new corporate account (and sometimes even *before* you have official sign-off) your work truly begins.

## Making the Most of Your New Account

Sales volume tends to follow the famous 80/20 Pareto Principle: It's not unusual for salespeople or companies to have as few as 20 percent of their accounts providing as much as 80 percent of their sales volume, whereas 80 percent of their accounts provide only 20 percent of their sales volume. If you are a small firm, these numbers may be even more extreme. That's both the beauty and the ugliness of large corporate accounts!

In 1999, we won a major account with the U.S. Air Force Reserve. That year, that account represented almost 20 percent of the year's gross revenue. Obviously, this account had a huge impact on every aspect of our business for the duration of the contract. But I am proud to say that we were able to manage the contract so well that we earned not just repeat business, but additional business over the years and a significant referral from the Air Force Reserve.

This brings me to my next major point: The top 20 percent of your accounts are the most likely to provide an ongoing source of sales for you. If you manage the top 20 percent of your clients effectively, you stand to gain tremendously in terms of expertise, growth, and reputation, and you'll be guaranteeing yourself steady, stable sources of income for years to come. The secret to doing this is finding ways to influence your clients' growth opportunities and creating a cooperative alliance between your firm and their corporation. The more vital you, personally, and your company as a whole become to an account, the more likely you are to eliminate current and future competition.

I have some scary news for you, though. A few years back, Walker Information Group published some research that said the following:

- 47 percent of decision makers plan to maintain existing relationships with their vendors.
- 27 percent are likely to continue doing business but are less than pleased with all the relationships.
- 21 percent are unhappy with, and therefore have a low intention of continuing, current relationships.
- 3 percent may not continue doing business, even though they're pleased with the relationships.

This essentially means that more than half of vendors are about to lose contracts with American corporations at any given time. The reasons? In most cases, it has to do with quality and delivery issues—we've talked a lot about that already. In other cases, it simply has to do with vendors mismanaging the account. You could be doing a wonderful job fulfilling your client's requirements, but meanwhile, your competitor has been telling the corporate buyer that his firm not only can handle the requirements but provide additional value as well. *You may lose the account not because you did anything wrong, but because you failed to make the most of your relationship with the buyer!*

## Developing Strategic Relationships

In previous chapters, I've talked about the importance of positioning yourself as a strategic resource for corporate and government buyers. As the story in the previous paragraph illustrates, positioning doesn't stop the moment you win the account! Just because you've won the account does not guarantee that your new client will be satisfied with your performance, that you'll win the account again when it's up for rebid, or that you'll be considered for additional business with the client.

### I submit to you the following truths:

1. Fixing immediate business pain is not based on relationships; it's based on competency and results.
2. Relationships are forged by fixing ongoing, meaningful problems.
3. True business relationships begin only after an organization has bought from you and has become an *obsessively pleased* customer—what we call a zealot—and not before.

How do these statements make you feel? When we talk about these points in our programs, we often get perplexed, and even angry, responses from the audience. For so many years, salespeople have been taught "relationship selling," and they've felt comfortable doing quarterly sales calls to their prospects and customers, taking with them a box of doughnuts and a vat of coffee. I'm not saying relationships with your corporate customers aren't desirable, but I *am* saying that some corporations don't *want* relationships with you, and even if they do, a mutually beneficial relationship takes time to build.

Let me put it another way: Your positioning will get you in the door. Your sales approach—intelligent questions and smart solutions—will win you the business. Your performance will keep you the business. Your positioning plus your sales approach plus your performance will earn you a relationship. Once you have a solid relationship, your goal should be to transform your satisfied customer into a true zealot for your firm. A zealot is more than a happy customer; a zealot will advocate for you whenever and wherever possible (even without being asked), essentially becoming an unpaid salesperson for you!

## Account Maintenance versus Account Management

Account management is a popular term in sales, but it seems to mean different things to different people. In our world, *account maintenance* encompasses all of the tactical, practical aspects of ensuring that activities associated with a particular project or contract go according to plan and are communicated properly to your customer. It's essentially the same thing as *project management*.

In contrast, *account management* is something that happens after you've shown your firm to be a strong provider or supplier over the course of at least one—and maybe several—projects for a corporation or government agency. According to the Strategic Account Management Association, "Installing a comprehensive strategic account management approach within a company requires significant financial investment, long-term focus, and multi-functional capabilities along with substantial restructuring of the sales organization."

### Account Maintenance

Before you can become a truly trusted resource and a valuable strategic partner, your firm will have to demonstrate that it is capable of delivering on all of the promises you've made during the sales process. I am shocked by how many small businesses have a lackadaisical approach to meeting and exceeding the requirements their clients have laid out for them. Account maintenance is a critical aspect of working with the giants (or any organization that provides you with large and/or complex projects)—it's far too important to overlook. We're talking far more than dealing in doughnuts and coffee when you make quarterly client visits, too.

This isn't a book about account maintenance or project management, but here are a few of the essential elements of managing projects from concept to conclusion:

1. **Establish an account manager.** Choose one person to be the primary point of contact with your client. You may have identified a primary point of contact during the process of submitting a request for proposal or during the contract negotiation phase. If not, do it immediately.

2. **Formally organize an account team.** Even if people play multiple roles, at least be clear on who is on the team. Anyone who has responsibility for fulfilling any aspect of the customer's requirements should be involved.

3. **Communication structure.** Poor communication is the single most common reason projects develop delays, encounter other problems, or fail. A few questions to answer:

   - Who on your team is authorized to communicate directly with your client? What level of authority do they have?

   - If problems arise, who is responsible for communicating issues with the client?

   - Who has the authority to make changes to the scope of work?

   - How often will the account team meet? Will the client have a representative at these meetings?

4. **Be "planful."** Again, there's a Pareto Principle: If you invest about 80 percent of your account maintenance effort on preparation and careful planning, you'll only have to spend about 20 percent on the actual work. Better planning always results in less work and better results.

5. **Executing and tracking.** If you're working on a complex project, I highly recommend using some sort of project management software application that's visible to everyone on the project team. As part of your planning process,

establish milestones and assign responsibility and authority to specific team members for accomplishing key tasks.
Track progress in as close to real time as possible so you
can head off problems and take advantage of being ahead of
schedule.

6. **Follow-up and lessons learned.** Virtually every project
has a snafu. When the project is complete, do a debrief.
Include everyone who had a role in the project—if the client
is willing, include their personnel as well. This should be
a no-blame meeting with no finger-pointing, but rather a
constructive discussion of how to avoid problems on future
projects.

## Account Management

Many years ago, we earned a fairly significant piece of business
with a firm that manufactures compressed-air and gas technology. We provided a customized sales training program for our
client's sales team, and they thought so highly of it they wanted to
offer the training experience to their distributor network. One of
our most seasoned and knowledgeable salespeople worked closely
with the client's representative to craft a sales training program
that could be rolled out to the company's entire distributor network. We collaborated with our client on every aspect of the sales
training program: developing a customized program, designing
incentive packages to encourage distributor sales reps to attend,
hosting a program registration Web site, training trainers, and
providing program reinforcement options.

The program was a huge success, and not only did our client
call on us to do a similar program the following year, but several other distributor networks got wind of the idea and called
us to design similar programs for them. We handled our initial project with our client—a two-and-a-half-day customized
training program—so well that it led to significant additional

business. Then, we managed the larger program rollout so well that it led to additional business with our client's clients and peer organizations.

When did our role shift from basic project management—account maintenance—to account management? When the client asked us to help them design a distributor sales program. Before that point, we were "just" a sales training firm doing its best to deliver an educational experience that had measurable results for our client. At the point our client asked for additional assistance, it became clear that we had truly differentiated ourselves in their minds and exhibited greater-than-average understanding of their needs and their distributors' requirements and desires. At that moment, we had to begin practicing both account maintenance (ensuring that each project we were assigned by our client ran smoothly) and account management (ensuring that we and our client collaborated effectively for our mutual long-term gain). And guess what? They're still one of our best clients, nine years and counting!

As we've suggested, account management encompasses more than account maintenance. Account management is all about strategically aligning yourself and your company with your key corporate accounts so that you are invaluable to them—both now and in the future. Superior account managers differentiate themselves by:

- **Taking control of their key and strategic accounts.** They don't miss anything—they take an active interest in the success of each account and pay close attention to the myriad factors that affect their clients' businesses each day.
- **Selling at consistently strong margins.** Underpricing hurts everything about your business. It undervalues your product or service and signals to your prospects and clients that you may be cutting corners or offering a lesser product than your competition. And remember: money you lose by

selling at low margins can never be made up in additional volume.

- **Being value creators, not just value communicators.** Provide vital, valuable, and meaningful information for your key contacts every time you meet. Seek to provide this information even when you are not trying to make a sale—it will be that much more valuable!

- **Understanding not only their clients' needs, but their clients' customers' requirements.** This is so critical, and yet so few salespeople get it. It's not enough to understand what your clients need and want—if you're going to be an innovative, essential resource for them, you've got to have some serious insight into what motivates *their* customers to buy from them.

- **Communicating effectively at all levels inside of accounts.** Understanding the roles and responsibilities of key personnel within your client's organization will help you uncover their requirements and motivations (needs and wants), which will enable you to target your messages to address each individual's unique concerns and desires.

## Returning to the Critical Roles of Quality and Delivery

In Chapter 2, we discussed the two most essential traits giant corporations and government agencies are looking for in their suppliers: the ability to provide quality products and services and the capacity to deliver them on time. I'd like to return to these issues, because they aren't just what helps a company decide to do business with you once, they're the "make or break" factors that determine whether they continue to do business with you. If you have tight control over quality and delivery—and visibility into these processes—the giants are far more likely to consider giving your firm additional responsibilities. Quality and delivery are essential to good account maintenance, and systems for tracking them will provide you a wealth of information that will help you be an active, engaged account manager.

A formal quality assurance program indicates to corporate and government buyers that you consider quality to be a vital factor and that you have taken the time to think through and implement an effective quality control system. Buyers will expect to review your written quality assurance plan, and they will often visit your facility and request access to your online systems so they may observe the plan in action.

Sure, your positioning is important, and your contacts within the giant's organization should perceive you as a strategic resource. But all of that positioning is for naught if your firm doesn't back up your marketing and sales promises with impressive day-to-day performance. Particularly if you sell a product, your large clients will need to see that there are systems in place to ensure that the products you are providing them consistently and reliably meet the standards of quality they require. There are many well-publicized quality programs that you can access on your own, but in general, they include:

- An organization chart
- Documentation, records, and corrective action procedures (often online)
- Measuring and test equipment
- Process control
- Indication of inspection status

Quality control has always been considered the arena of manufacturing—measuring the quality of manufactured products against definable standards. But increasingly, service providers are being asked to provide evidence of quality control, too—and they have even more of a stake in developing a quality assurance program because their outcomes and products are more difficult to measure. We see this regularly in our work with clients, who want to be able to document proof that their investment in sales and sales management training paid off. Components of a service-oriented quality assurance plan include the following:

- A quality assurance director
- A procedure for checking work in progress
- A time-management and time-monitoring system (particularly if you bill hourly for services)
- Internal and external communication forms

Because a service may be difficult to measure, it is all the more important that you plan and outline your efforts to do so. You will have more flexibility than a manufacturer in both designing your plan and implementing it, and your propensity toward innovation in quality control will stand you in good stead with potential and existing corporate customers. The key question to ask your clients is: "How will you and I know when the job has been done correctly?"

Delivery is an essential component of quality, isn't it? If you can't deliver the quality products and services you promise, you're not following through on your commitment. For a majority of products and services, on-time delivery is a prerequisite for success. Whether you provide a product or a service, you should be prepared for audits of your quality and delivery—both on a regular, scheduled basis and through unscheduled checks.

## Is Every Account Automatically Qualified for More Sales?

In the ideal world, every large project with a corporate giant would yield additional opportunities. The bad news is that's just not reality. The good news, though, is that it's not that hard to determine which giants have potential for you and which don't. And it's also not that hard to put yourself in the position of making more business opportunities for your firm.

Let's look first at how to qualify your giant prospects for additional sales. Here are five characteristics you should look for.

1. The client has a need for additional products, solutions, or processes, and the client's representatives have made it clear that they're amenable to them.

2. You have a relationship with one or more decision makers who have the legitimate authority and financial ability to buy or commit to additional offerings from your company.

3. Your client's decision makers have a relative sense of urgency about making additional buying decisions.

4. The client's team members trust you and your firm as the result of your proven availability, predictable delivery, quality, service, and commitment.

5. Client decision makers will listen to what you have to say on the basis of your proven track record as a business ally.

Do any of your existing large accounts meet all five of these criteria? If so, I hope you've positioned yourself well and are in regular communication with your client's decision makers about any project you could play a part in. If not, it's not a lost cause. It just means that you won't likely make a follow-up sale immediately, and you'll have some work to do in terms of continually positioning yourself as a value resource for client personnel.

## Tips for Maximizing Your Accounts with the Giants

In some cases, a giant corporation's small business liaison's office does a superior job keeping its suppliers and potential suppliers in the loop about potential projects. However, in most cases, it's going to be up to you to work with these individuals to find, suggest, and develop opportunities for yourself and to stay ahead of your competitors in the "value-adding" game. Years of experience and observation have given me some practical insights into how to do this:

- Do your best to know when to move from sales status to account maintenance status to account management status. Assuming the "partner" role too soon is presumptuous and risky. Take the time to demonstrate that you are interested in your client's welfare, not just your own.

- Provide valuable, insightful information for your key contacts every time you meet. Reciprocity will then make them want to do the same for you.

- Create a vivid picture of what you can do to help your client's organization in ways above and beyond what you're doing now. Your goal is to ensure that your client readily sees you as an essential stakeholder in their organization.

- Be 110-percent dependable and earn the right to achieve preferred vendor or supplier status. Make your key contacts look good.

- Educate your key contacts about any impending upgrades, new product introductions, research and development plans, and other developments. Allow them to anticipate how to apply your products or services in new, different ways.

- Always, always keep your key contacts in the loop and give them full credit for "finding you." Make them want to refer you to others in their organization—and at other companies—whose problems you can solve.

- Probe your key contacts to determine how receptive they are toward discussing future directions for their organization. If they're receptive, do it. If not, work on your relationship until they are willing to do so.

- Identify and make contact with the people who have access to—and shape—strategic plans for your clients' organization. Remember that other divisions, regions, or departments of the company may be able to use your products or services.

Positioning yourself is not a one-time deal for any salesperson or company owner, something to be conscientiously worked toward before your first contract and never thought of again. At every step of your interaction with a new client, you have a new opportunity to position yourself, your firm, and your products or services in a positive light. All too often, salespeople forget about an account once they win a piece of business and move on to the next big prospect.

Remember: You could be sitting on acres of diamonds with an existing account. There's no substitute for "walking the halls" with a supremely satisfied customer and being treated not just as a valuable resource but as a respected business partner. In that role, you'll be among the first to learn of new business opportunities, and you may be the first to discover a need or want your firm can fulfill for your client. You'll make yourself into a value creator, not just a value communicator, and your competitors will never catch up if you do it well.

## Conclusion

So often, I hear people say that good salespeople are just "naturals" at it—they make it look so easy. Yes, there are gifted salespeople who seem to have a sixth sense about how to approach prospects and customers sincerely and effectively. But the truth is that success at sales is far more than being a "people person," being well-connected, or any of the other attributes usually cited. Sales—especially to giant corporations and government agencies—requires a special blend of confidence, self management, empathy, motivation, and strategic and tactical skills that *can* be developed. It may take work, but I believe that if you're reading this book, you have it in you.

For many of us, selling to giants is a wonderful challenge that has huge potential rewards if we approach it with the right attitude and skill set. Most of what you've read in this book is the result of 30-plus years of "in the trenches" selling on my part and observing what has worked—and not worked—for me and others. At The Brooks Group, we've learned not just how contracts from large organizations will transform our small business but also—and probably even more significantly, how our small business can have the power to transform large organizations.

If you, as a small business owner or salesperson, can keep that concept in mind, selling to the giants will be a lot easier for you. Constantly reminding yourself that your firm's small(er) size has little or nothing to do with the value you can add to a giant organization will help you combat any fears you have of selling to the "Goliaths" against your "Goliath" competitors. As I hope I've shown you in this book, there are countless reasons why large organizations want to work with companies like yours and ours, and just as many reasons you should pursue these giant prospects.

The benefits of providing services and products to the giants can be great, both for your organization and you, personally. We at The Brooks Group wish you all the best in exceeding your own highest expectations!

## Critical Points from This Chapter

- If you make the best of your first contract with a giant company or agency, it can be the best opportunity you've ever seen—but if you bungle it, it can be the biggest headache and wasted investment you've ever faced.

- Sales volume tends to follow the 80/20 Pareto Principle: It's not unusual for a company to have as few as 20 percent of their accounts providing as much as 80 percent of their sales volume. These top 20 percent of your accounts are the most likely to provide an ongoing source of sales for you, too.

- It's all too common for firms to lose accounts not because they did anything wrong but because they failed to make the most of their relationship with the buyer.

- Fixing immediate business pain is not based on relationships, it's based on competency and results. Relationships are forged by fixing ongoing, meaningful problems. True business relationships begin only after an organization has bought from you and has become an obsessively pleased customer—what we call a zealot—and not before.

- Your positioning plus your sales approach plus your performance will earn you a relationship.

- Account maintenance encompasses all the practical, tactical aspects of ensuring that activities associated with a particular project or contract go according to plan.

- Account management is something that happens after you've shown your firm to be a strong provider or supplier over the course of at least one—and maybe several—projects or contracts.

- Superior account managers:
  - take control of their key and strategic accounts.
  - sell at consistently strong margins.
  - are value creators, not just value communicators.
  - understand not just their clients' needs but also their clients' customers' requirements.

(*continued*)

(*continued*)

- communicate effectively at all levels inside of accounts.
- Quality and delivery are essential to good account maintenance, and systems for tracking them will provide you with a wealth of information that will help you be an active, engaged account manager.
- Your clients will need to see that there are systems in place to ensure that the products you are providing them consistently and reliably meet the standards of quality they require.
- The five characteristics of an account that's qualified for more sales:
    1. Account stakeholders have a need for additional solutions, and they've made it clear they're amenable to them.
    2. You have a relationship with decision makers who have the legitimate authority and financial ability to buy or commit to additional offerings from your company.
    3. Your client's decision makers have a relative sense of urgency about making additional buying decisions.
    4. The client's team members trust you and your firm as the result of your proven availability, predictable delivery, quality, service, and commitment.
    5. Client decision makers will listen to what you have to say on the basis of your proven track record as a business ally.
- It's up to you to find, suggest, and develop opportunities for yourself and stay ahead of your competitors in the "value-adding" game.

# Index